Sign Language Recognition

Dr.R. Elakkiya

Published by

BONFRING®
Intellectual Integrity

Sign Language Recognition

9 788195 162628 >

ISBN 978-81-951626-2-8

Author

Dr.R. Elakkiya

Bonfring

309, 2nd Floor, 5th Street Extension, Gandhipuram,

Coimbatore-641 012.

Tamilnadu, India.

E-mail: info@bonfring.org

Website: www.bonfring.org

Overview

This book presents a Sign Modelling Framework for Automatic Sign Language Recognition from continuous video sequences consisting of isolated words and signed sentences. This book addresses three major issues of automatic sign language recognition namely (i) the importance of discriminative feature extraction and selection, (ii) handling epentheses movements and segmentation ambiguities, and (iii) automatic recognition of large vocabulary sign sentences and signer adaptation in a single subunit sign modelling framework. Hence, this book focuses on the three major contributions for addressing the above issues.

The first contribution presented in this book is the feature extraction and selection technique to identify the best features for recognizing the signs. Hence, a novel Bi-fold Bayesian Parallel Hidden Markov Model (BPaHMM) is introduced to classify the manual and non-manual features of sign languages from continuous video sequences. A discriminative feature selection strategy based on the information gain is introduced to select the important features and to reduce the feature space and computation time.

The second contribution features an Enhanced Dynamic Programming (EDP) framework to handle the epentheses movements present in between the adjacent signs and the segmentation ambiguities in continuous sign sentences. A Subunit Multi-stream Parallel Hidden Markov Model (SMP-HMM) is introduced to model the subunits, besides a spatiotemporal clustering to dynamically prune the epentheses movements without any explicit or implicit modelling.

The third contribution of this research work is the development of a subunit sign modelling framework to automatically recognize the large vocabulary of multilingual isolated signs and continuous sentences under different signer variations and illuminations. Based on the selected discriminative features, the subunit sign modelling framework is introduced and sign lexicon is constructed for spatial subunits and temporal subunits where the spatial subunits includes hand shape and the temporal subunits includes velocity and position using BPaHMM. To model these subunits, SMP-HMM is used to train these subunits using Viterbi and Baum-Welch algorithms. The recognition begins with the emission probabilities from each node of HMM states.

Finally, this book has evaluated and experimented subjectively and quantitatively with the real-time signing videos gathered from different corpora and different sign languages including American Sign Language Lexicon Video Dataset (ASLLVD), RWTH-BOSTON-104 (British Sign Language), RWTH-PHOENIX-Weather Dataset (German Sign Language) and self-captured videos (American Sign Language Sentences). The results of the experiments have proved that the proposed subunit sign framework can recognize large vocabulary corpora, adapt signer independence and handle the epentheses movements with high accuracy. Extensive experimentation was also carried out to compare the proposed framework with four other subunit level sign models and two whole sign level model. The proposed framework shows promising results when compared with other existing approaches. Also, it is proved that the scalability of the system remains constant while increasing the sign vocabulary and the proposed approach is more reliable, and is efficient enough to adapt to real-time constraints.

Acknowledgement

The research was funded by the Science and Engineering Research Board (SERB), India under Start-up Research Grant (SRG)/2019–2021 (Grant no. SRG/2019/001338). We thank SASTRA Deemed University for providing infrastructural support to conduct the research. And also, we thank all the students for their contribution in collecting the sign videos and the successful completion of the ISL-CSLTR corpus. We would like to thank Navajeevan, Residential School for the Deaf, College of Spl. D.Ed & B.Ed, Vocational Centre, and Child Care & Learning Centre, Ayyalurimetta, Nandyal, Andhra Pradesh, India for their support and contribution.

My first and foremost acknowledgment must go to my supervisor Dr.K. Selvamani, Assistant Professor, Department of Computer Science and Engineering, CEG Campus, Anna University, Chennai. He was the one who persuaded me to continue my graduate studies and inspired me with his enthusiasm as well as his experience on research.

I also thank my family members, friends, colleagues and supporters throughout the work and my gratitude goes to all of them. I owe special gratitude to my lovable kid Yadhoorsh Elayaraja for his patience during the completion of this book. My last, and most heartfelt, acknowledgment must go to my husband Mr.K. Elayaraja. He was always there for me, with his love, patience and support, when I needed the most.

Dr.R. Elakkiya

TABLE OF CONTENTS

List of Tables

LIST OF FIGURES

LIST OF SYMBOLS AND ABBREVIATIONS

AAM	-	Active Appearance Model
ABPNN	-	Annealing Back Propagation Neural Network
ANN	-	Artificial Neural Networks
ArSL	-	Arabic Sign Language
ASL	-	American Sign Language
ASLLVD	-	American Sign Language Lexicon Video Dataset
ASLRC	-	Automatic Sign Language Recognition and Classification
AUSLAN	-	Australian Sign Language
BPaHMM	-	Bayesian Parallel Hidden Markov Model
BSL	-	Brazilian Sign Language
CDFD	-	Combined Discriminative Feature Detectors
CHMM	-	Coupled Hidden Markov Model
CNN	-	Convolutional Neural Networks
CSL	-	Chinese Sign Language
CSLR	-	Continuous Sign Language Recognition
CSR	-	Continuous Sentence Recognition
CRF	-	Conditional Random Field
DASL	-	Dictionary of American Sign Language
DDTW	-	Derivative Dynamic Time Warping
Dez	-	Designator
DIST-SBHMM	-	Discriminative State-Space Tying-Segmentally Boosted Hidden Markov Model
DNN	-	Deep Neural Network
DTW	-	Dynamic Time Warping
EDP	-	Enhanced Dynamic Programming
EM	-	Epentheses Movements
FHMM	-	Factorial Hidden Markov Model
FSM	-	Finite State Machines
GB	-	Gesture Base
GMM	-	Gaussian Mixture Models
GR	-	Gesture Recognition

GRFNN	-	Gesture Recognition Fuzzy Neural Network
GSL	-	German Sign Language
GTHMM	-	Gesture Threshold Hidden Markov Model
HamNoSys	-	Hamburg Notation System
HCRF	-	Hierarchical Conditional Random Field
HMI	-	Human-Machine Interaction
HMM	-	Hidden Markov Model
HS	-	Hand Shape
HSV	-	Hue Saturation Value
IMU	-	Inertial Measurement Unit
IOHMM	-	Input / Output Hidden Markov Model
ISL	-	Indian Sign Language
ISR	-	Isolated Sign Recognition
KNN	-	K-Nearest Neighbor
LDCRF	-	Latent Dynamic Conditional Random Fields
LED	-	Light Emitting Diode
LMC	-	Leap Motion Controller
MAP	-	Maximum Posterior Estimation
MEC	-	Minimum Entropy Clustering
ML	-	Machine Learning
MLLR	-	Maximum Linear Likelihood Regression
MLP	-	Multi-Layered Perceptron
MLPNN	-	Multi-layered Perceptron Neural Network
NN	-	Neural Networks
PaHMM	-	Parallel Hidden Markov Model
PCA	-	Principal Component Analysis
PHMM	-	Parametric Hidden Markov Model
PSL	-	Polish Sign Language
RNN	-	Recurrent Neural Network
RVM	-	Relevance Vector Machine
SCRF	-	Segmental Conditional Random Field
SDGC	-	Supervised-Dynamic Gesture Classification
SDTW	-	Statistical Dynamic Time Warping

SIFT	-	Scale Invariant Feature Transform
Sig	-	Signation
SL	-	Sign Language
SLR	-	Sign Language Recognition
SMP-HMM	-	Subunit Multi-stream Parallel Hidden Markov Model
SOFM	-	Self Organizing Feature Map
SOM	-	Self Organizing Map
SRN	-	Simple Recurrent Network
SSGC	-	Supervised-Static Gesture Classification
SURF	-	Speeded Up Robust Feature
SU-F	-	Subunit Frames
SU-IMH	-	Subunit and Imagenet-Hand motion
SU-noST	-	Subunit without Spatial and Temporal Feature
SVM	-	Support Vector Machine
S/T	-	Spatial/Temporal
SW-1	-	Whole Sign-1
SW-2	-	Whole Sign-2
Tab	-	Tabula
TDNN	-	Time Delay Neural Network
THMM	-	Threshold Hidden Markov Model
TMA	-	Template Matching Algorithm
TMM	-	Transition Movement Model
TP	-	Temporal Position
TV	-	Temporal Velocity
UDGC	-	Unsupervised Dynamic Gesture Classification
USGC	-	Unsupervised Static Gesture Classification
WDTW	-	Weighted Dynamic Time Warping

CHAPTER I

1. Introduction

1.1. Sign Language

Sign Language (SL) serves as a communication medium among the deaf and hard of hearing society. Sign language habitually contributes considerable resemblances to their relevant spoken words but sign language has its own structure and grammar and it varies according to the fluency of signing. Sign language should not be considered as body language just because it is another way of non-linguistic communication because general linguistics considers both signed and spoken language as different types of natural language.

Sign language communication involves in visual conveying of meaning instead of spoken words. This communication involves the simultaneous combination of both manual and non-manual means of expressions. The manual parameters include hand shape, hand position, hand orientation, hand trajectories and arms movements while the non-manual parameters include facial expressions, head and body postures, mouth and gaze directions. All these expressions together convey the intended meaning and information of the signer's in terms of visual projection for the deaf and hard of hearing people.

Sign Languages have been developed wherever the deaf communities are present. SL is not only used by the deaf and hearing impaired community but also it is used by the hearing community who are all not able to speak or having some trouble with spoken language due to some other disabilities like augmentative communication. Sign languages are not similar in most of the countries and they vary for each country. Also, each and every country has its own native sign language and some countries have more than one sign language. Also, some sign languages have obtained legal recognition whereas the other sign languages do not have such recognition.

1.2. Sign Language Recognition

Automatic Recognition of Sign Language is an important issue for enabling communication with sensory and gustatory impaired people. In Gesture Recognition (GR) hierarchy, Sign Languages are acceptably considered as the topmost essential gesture to be recognized. Such importance induces the automatic recognition of signs as an evolving multi-disciplinary research to confront some areas including Human-Computer Interaction, Pattern Recognition, Computer Vision, Fuzzy Systems, Neural Networks, Machine Learning and other fields.

Sign language recognition poses a peculiar challenge due to the visual analysis of hand gestures and the multimodal nature of sign gestures. Albeit, sign languages are complex in structure with their own syntax, grammar, phonology and morphology, they vary in structure from spoken language. Generally, spoken language structure uses words in a sequential order whereas sign language uses several body movements in parallel. Therefore, linguistics behaviour of sign languages also varies due to the existence of several components including head movements and facial expressions along with the hand movements.

Even in this computer era, there exist certain limitations in technology for traditional Human-Machine Interaction (HMI). Henceforth, there is a strong need for research in the field of human-computer interaction will become essential to real life. One of the most important research areas in HMI is sign language recognition. The main objective of SLR is to translate signs into text or speech, thereby the communication between the impaired and healthy society can be initiated.

According to HMI, user interaction with computers would be more practical and natural; it seems that the development of recognition of speech and gesture is all more needed now. Hence, research on these recognitions made a new shift to understanding the gesture commands to enable communication in noisy environments where the spoken language does not work. In turn, leads to the development of sign language recognition paradigm to help the hearing-impaired society.

Research in the field of Automatic Sign Language Recognition and Classification (ASLRC) has mainly focused on two dimensions namely Isolated Sign Recognition (ISR) and Continuous Sentence Recognition (CSR). Isolated word recognition involves in recognizing a single hand gesture that the signer performs to convey the information whereas the continuous recognition involves identifying the sequence of gestures signed by the signer one after the other. Among these two recognition problems, CSR is quite different because in hand gesture recognition it is considered as gesture spotting and in sign language recognition the problem is considered as a co-articulation problem. The co-articulation problem makes recognition more complex because the ascendant sign affects the descendant sign and the transition between the signs i.e. Epentheses Movements (EM) ought to be explicitly or implicitly modelled to integrate into the recognition systems.

Research on ASLRC started with Device-Based approaches using sensors and trackers. Albeit these approaches produce accurate results in tracking and pointing the gestures, the signer loses their natural way of signing by constantly required to wearing burdensome devices or trackers on their hands. On the other hand, Vision-Based approaches in sign-language recognition provide a user-friendly environment for signers. However, this approach also faces several challenges in CSR that are handling occlusion of hands over face, co-articulation problem, segmenting, detecting hand and finger configuration and modelling the transition movements between the signs. In order to overcome these challenges, many vision-based approaches use different coloured gloves on hands or colour markers for fingers. Despite all these, the marker-free recognition of sign language detection, recognition and classification in cluttered and unrestricted environments is the tranquil open research problem.

1.3. Motivation

Automatic speech recognition systems are now advanced and have developed to the extent of being available commercially, but ASLRC is still at its outset to explore. All commercial interface translation systems are human-oriented and are considered to be more expensive because of the requirements of more experienced interpreters.

In general, ASLR algorithms are developed to classify accurately and to understand the meanings of the continuous sequence of signed sentences and isolated words. Several researchers have considered the GR problem as sign language recognition. Conversely, SL is apart from just a collection of detailed gestures. Henceforth, the research has consequently hitherto correctly labelling the given sign or sign sentences from the possible set of signs based on optimal feature extraction and classification methods.

Sign languages are seen as a multi-channel mode for conveying the meaningful information via more than one node at once. Linguistic studies of SLR are still in its infancy and it is obviously known that many of the approaches proposed for speech recognition are also not suitable for SLR techniques. In addition, the availability of public data sets is also limited in both qualitatively and quantitatively, which interprets the conventional computer vision and machine learning algorithms as derisory for building the effective classifiers.

A SL interpreter is a professional, translates a spoken language into signs and sign language into spoken words. In order to assist the communication deaf and hard-of-hearing people, SL interpreters are quite often used. Sign languages are different from any spoken language because they have their own syntax and structure; hence this interpretation involves substantial effort on the part of the interpreters. Albeit, SL interpreters who are able to translate between sign and natural languages are not usually paired and are available less frequently.

In automatic speech recognition, there are formal dictionaries available to construct the spoken word from the subset of phonemes. But in case of automatic SLR, there is a lack of such dictionaries available to construct the subunits. The available dictionaries of subunits are based on linguistic models which include Stokoe system, Liddell and Johnson Movement-Hold model, the Hamburg Notation system and the SignWriting.

All these models use manual annotation to locate these subunits which are tedious and very time-consuming process. On the other hand, there are models which used data-driven approaches motivated to form the basic units without manual interventions. However, these models do not lead to any standard subunit dictionaries available for reuse. Therefore, all these together still render the research in automatic SLR for subunit modelling a challenging one.

1.4. Sign Language Linguistics

The main objective of SLR system is to recognize large vocabulary under unrestricted environments which would make the communication easy between the hearings impaired community and normal hearing people. Sign language linguistics is mainly composed of three components; namely manual signals, non-manual signals and finger spelling. Manual signals are made only with hand gestures employing hand shape, position, orientation and motion trajectories, Non-manual signals are those made with facial expressions, body postures and head positions which are used as a part of the sign or to modify the meaning of a manual signals, and finger spelling are the gestures which spell out the words as individual letters using local verbal language.

An ultimate system that contains this linguistics would take a sign language video as input and texts sign language sentences as output. Unsurprisingly, this is a generalization because sign languages are also intricate in nature like any other spoken languages which comprises an abundant number of signs; every sign differs from the other/s by minute changes in manual or non-manual signals. Generally, a sign language has its own semantic structure and syntax which are formulated using manual and non-manual parameters, sequential and simultaneous aspect patterns and linear and spatial arrangements of signs. Sign linguistics can also be depicted using chremes like phonemes in spoken languages at the subunit level. These chremes predetermine several cues of the sign. Unlike, speech recognition it is not mandatory that they should occur sequentially but they can be simultaneously combined to illustrate a sign.

1.4.1. Manual Linguistics

Manual linguistics is the essential component that are required to recognize the sign language. The manual signals are further divided in terms of three major components namely hand shape, hand motion and place of articulation. When considered the manual signals without incorporating the non-manual components, it is treated as the subset of elements of gestural communication. Also, the manual cues are highly structured, restricted and more complex concerning the two-handed signs. Albeit, the manual cue analysis is treated as a part of gesture communication and it needs more personalized methods in case of solving large-vocabulary sign recognition system, or in analyzing the correlation of hands. Many of the existing approaches in SLR focus on hand postures that are the static hand shapes, ignoring the fact that many sign languages contain signs with motion invariants. When it comes to large-vocabulary recognition system, it is highly infeasible to recognize all the signs only with the help of static postures. Figure 1.1 shows the various methods of extracting manual cues in SLR systems.

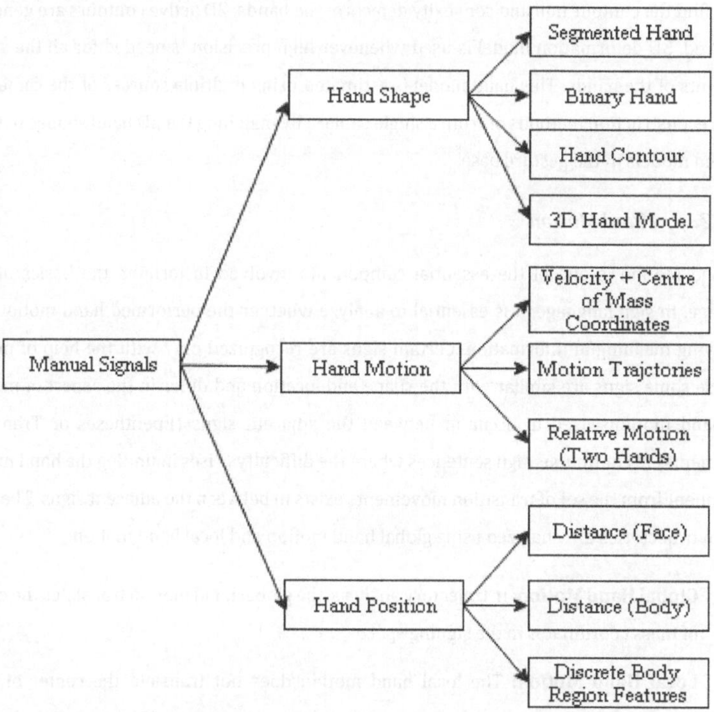

Figure 1.1: Extraction of Manual Signal in Sign Language Recognition

1.4.1.1. *Hand Shape*

Hand shape is the most important manual component involved in sign languages. Analyzing hand shape with a high degree of freedom is considered as highly a challenging task. For gesture-controlled devices, analyzing hand shapes is easier since they use only a limited number of simple hand shapes. However in sign languages, the vocabulary of the system grows larger and the probable discrimination of hand shapes makes the task very exigent and highly complicated.

In real time applications, the analysis of hand shapes involves in extracting manual features, the 2D hand images must be considered for they are simple and demand less computation time. Extraction of these manual features includes region-based descriptors and shape-based descriptors. The region-based descriptors constitute moments and moments-based invariants also called as grid descriptors whereas the shape-based features include Fourier descriptors or Curvature descriptors.

To find the contour hull and convexity defects of the hands, 2D active contours are generally preferred. 3D deformation model is used whenever high precision is needed for all the angles and joints of the hands. This hand model is estimated using multiple sources of the camera by using reconstruction methods or from a single camera by matching the 2D hand shapes with the 3D hand models in the gesture base.

1.4.1.2. Hand Motion

Hand Motion is one of the essential components involved in forming the basics of sign language. In sign language, it is essential to analyze whether the performed hand motions are conveying meaningful information. Certain signs are recognized only with the help of motion because some signs are similar with the shape and location and differ in the aspect of motion. The hand motions used to occur in between the adjacent signs (Epentheses or Transition Movements) in continuous sign sentences where the difficulty arises in finding the hand motion component from the set of transition movements exists in between the adjacent signs. The hand motion trajectories are analyzed using global hand motion and local hand motion.

a) **Global Hand Motion:** In trajectory analysis, the global hand motion translates the center of mass coordinates in the signing space.

b) **Local Hand Motion:** The local hand motion does not translate the center of mass coordinates or it occurs as the finger configuration changes in the signing space. For local hand motion, the changes in hand shape should be analyzed in detail because even minor changes in hand shape will convey some meaningful information.

The initial step in hand trajectory analysis is identifying the cartesian coordinates for the center of mass (centroid) irrespective of the noise due to illumination under various occlusions.

For this, six different example signs namely SEARCH, DRINK, FAMILY, CLASS, ONION, APPLE from ASL dictionary (Ding & Martinez 2007) is chosen as shown in Figure 1.2 to illustrate the minor variation in manual cues with respect to these signs and shows the importance of the manual components involved in sign language recognition. Figure 1.2 (a) signs with same hand shape but different hand motion, (b) signs with same motion but different hand shape and (c) signs with same motion and same hand shape but different hand position.

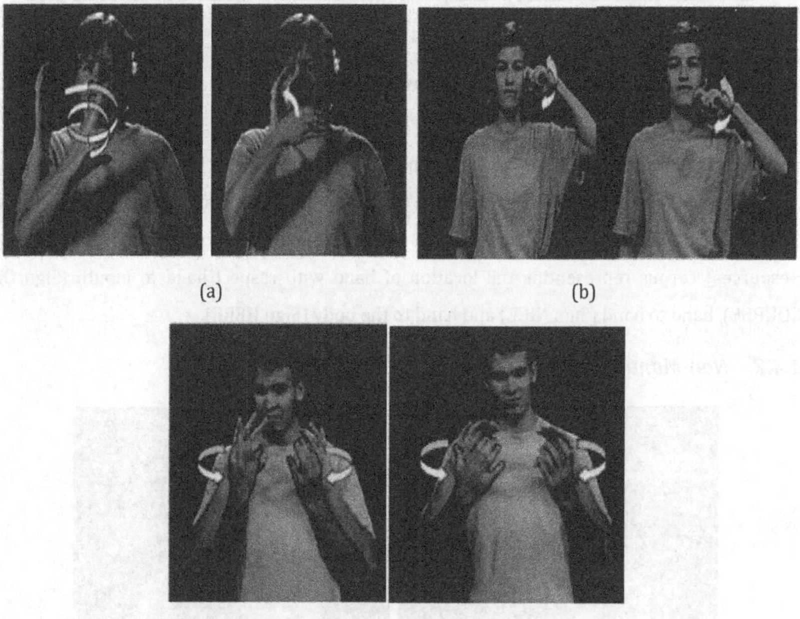

(a) (b)

(c)

Figure 1.2: Illustration of Manual Component in Different Shapes, Position and Motion

1.4.1.3. Hand Position

Hand position is another important modality in recognizing continuous sentences. The location of the hands in signing space with respect to the reference point from the centroid of the trajectories must be analyzed. The occurrences of the first and second position of the hand should be done in order to find the trajectory and to locate the hand in continuous video sequences. The first position of the hand in the current frame can be evaluated using the distance between the centroid of the trajectory and the starting reference point of the hand gesture.

(a) (b) (c)

Figure 1.3: Different Positions and Occlusions of Signs (a) Hand to Face (b) Hand to Hand and (c) Hand to Body

Similarly, the second position can be estimated using the distance between the occurrences of the starting point of the hand gesture in the frame and the current point of the gesture. Figure 1.3 shows three different signs from NCSLGR (National Centre for Sign Language and Gesture Resources) corpus representing the location of hand with respect hand to mouth (Sign OF COURSE), hand to hand (Sign NICE) and hand to the body (Sign HERE).

1.4.2. Non-Manual Linguistics

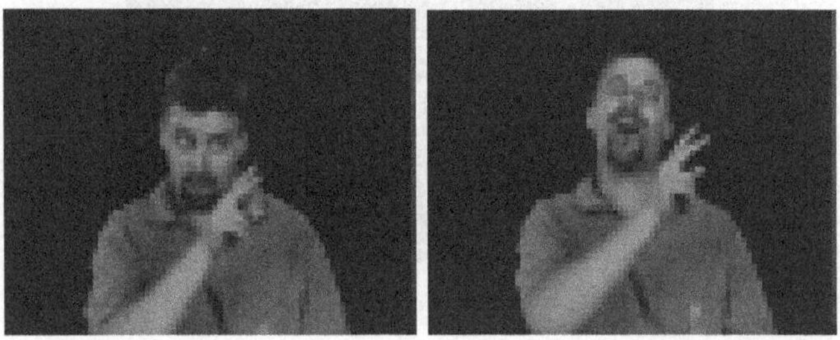

(a) (b)

Figure 1.4: Same Manual Cues but different Non-manual Expressions a) Sign Showing "ARE YOU READING" and b) Sign Showing "HAVE YOU READ"

A non-Manual signal in SLR plays a vital role in conveying the significant amount of meaningful information in addition to manual signals. The most useful non-manual cues are Facial Expressions, Lip Movements and Head Pose Estimation. The non-manual cue expressions are raising or lowering the eyebrows, eye gaze, head nods and shakes, nose wrinkling, lip movements and different degrees of eye aperture. These cues will manoeuvre as an indicator and provides supplementary information to work as modulation function which involved in adding lexical and semantic properties of signs. Combination of these facial expressions and head pose estimation helps in understanding certain grammatical status which includes question types, negations, when clauses and relative clauses.

Few researches have concentrated on estimating the body pose while narrating dialogues and stories. Similarly, facial expressions namely happiness, sadness, anger, fear, disgust and surprise are also used to analyze the sign recognition. Few signs in ASL are disambiguated only with the help of such expressions and the recognition only be accomplished with the lip shapes. Even though lip reading is a well-established field of research, which is also aided its importance in sign and speech recognition too. For example, the signs in figure 1.4, a)"ARE YOU READING" and b)"HAVE YOU READ" from NCSLGR corpus shows the same sign "READ" but the difference can only be seen in their facial expressions.

1.5. Sign Notations

Speech recognition has formal dictionaries available to construct a spoken word from a subset of phonemes but a sign language does not have any standards or traditional writing systems. Sign language for hard-of-hearing people has unique features of iconicity when compared to a spoken language that has an arbitrary one. Therefore, to write sign language description, photographs, line drawings and structural illustrations have been used to process the small set of signs.

1.5.1. Stokoe Notation

Stokoe Notation (Stokoe et al. 1976) was the first sign writing notation that has been available in sign language. The Dictionary of American Sign Language (DASL) based on linguistic Principles uses phonemic scripts. It was designed by William Stokoe using Latin letters and numerals for American Sign Language. In DASL, each sign is denoted by using three graphemes that distinguish one sign from the other and the term is denoted as "aspects".

The phonological graphemes are broken down into three elements namely hand configuration (which makes the hand sign), place of articulation (in which location the sign is made) and movements (where the actions of hand or hands begin). These three elements are named as the designator (dez) for the active hand configuration, the place of articulation as tabula (tab) and the movement as signation (sig). Generally, there are 55 graphemes in Stokoe notation 19 for dez, 24 for tab and 12 for sig. A single sign is represented in the order tab, dez and sig and written horizontally from left to right. Table 1.1 lists the sample Stokoe notations used to denote the signs.

Table 1.1: Lists of Sample Stokoe Notations

Notation	Symbol	Description
Tab	0	neutral location
	H	face, or whole head (symbol is superimposed ⌒ and ◡)
	U	forehead, brow, or upper face
	M	eyes, nose, or mid face
	L	lips, chin, or lower face
Dez	A	fist (as ASL 'a', 's', or 't')
	B	flat hand (as ASL 'b' or '4')
	5	spread hand (as ASL '5')
	C	cupped hand (as ASL 'c', or more open)
	3	vehicle classifier hand, thumb + index + middle fingers (as ASL '3')
Sig	D^	moving upward
	Dv	moving downward
	D^r	moving up and down
	D>	to the dominant side
	D+	Cross
	Do	Enter

Stokoe sign written forms are 55 symbols based on the three aspects which is predominantly limited to linguistics and designed specifically for illustrating the use of hand gestures in sign language. This notation does not concentrate on facial expressions and other non-manual cues of sign languages. Conversely, this system was introduced as a dictionary for research purpose, not for general uses.

1.5.2. Hamburg Notation System

The Hamburg Notation System (HamNoSys) is a detailed phonetic-based sign description system anticipated as a detailed phonetic transcription system for research purposes but not designed for any specific sign language. For one hand sign, the HamNoSys notation consists of manual features (hand shape, hand orientation, hand location), non-manual features (eye gaze, facial expressions, mouth gestures and mouth postures) and hand trajectories (Sequential and Parallel). Similarly for double handed signs, usually the posture notations start with symmetry operator of the dominant hands where as it copies the notation of the non-dominant hand when it is properly specified. In double-handed signs, notations of non-manual features and trajectories are not obligatory. Figure 1.5 shows the HamNoSys notation (Hanke 2004) for manual and non-manual cues of single hand with trajectory information. HamNoSys transcription system consists of about 200 symbols representing signs of single and double hands at alphabetic level.

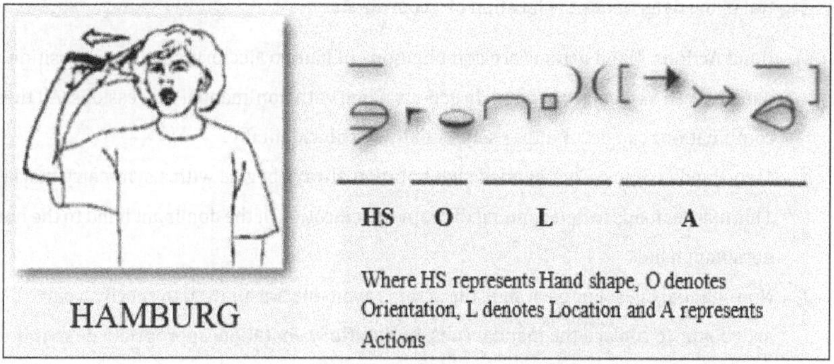

Figure 1.5: Hamburg Notation Systems

1.5.2.1. Hand Shape

In HamNoSys notation, hand shape symbols form the basic forms and diacritics for thumb location as well as for bending positions. In addition to thumb positions, hand shape deviations with respect to the position of other fingers or individual fingers are also specified. Figure 1.6 represents the hand shape information according to thumb position and bending.

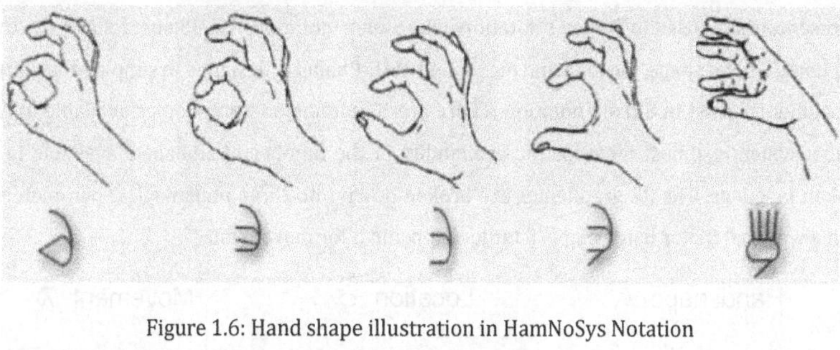

Figure 1.6: Hand shape illustration in HamNoSys Notation

1.5.2.2. Hand Orientation

Hand Orientation is described using two components namely extended index finger and palm orientation. The extended index finger represents two degrees of freedom whereas the palm orientation represents the third degree of freedom. At a distance of 45°, both components will be finely grained by providing sufficient symbols to determine 3D-orientation of the hands.

1.5.2.3. *Hand Location*

Hand location specification is determined using two components namely coronal plane and sagittal plane. Coronal Plane determines the location of x and y coordinates of the hand whereas the sagittal plane determines the location of z coordinate.

a) Hand Actions: Hand actions are combinations of hand trajectory, changes in position of hand as well as changes in hand directions along with non-manual expressions. All these combinations can occur either sequentially or coincidentally.
b) Two-Handed Signs: Two-handed sign notation always begins with a symmetry marker. This marker helps in determining the copy specification of the dominant hand to the non-dominant hand.
c) Non-manual Cues: For each sign, the actions available are allowed to specify a particular articulator to replace the manual cues. In HamNoSys notation, appropriate descriptions are available for head movements and shoulder shrugging along with facial circle to be harmonized with diacritics for eye and gaze movements, nose, cheeks and mouth movements.

1.5.3. *ASL-Phabet*

ASL-Phabet is a sign writing system designed by Dr Sam Supalla for American Sign Language (ASL) to educate the young impaired students. It is based on two sign notations namely SignFont and Stokoe notation. ASL-Phabet uses the symbols of SignFont and follows the grapheme representation as used in Stokoe's notation. Like Stokoe notation, ASL-Phabet follows the three graphemes: hand shape, location and movement. ASL-Phabet is designed to simplify the number of graphemes used in Stokoe notation. There are 32 numbers of graphemes available in ASL-Phabet which is almost ideal for the availability of the number of alphabets available in the spoken language. The 32 graphemes are broken down into three phonological parameters in such a way that 22 for hand shape, 5 for location and 5 for movement.

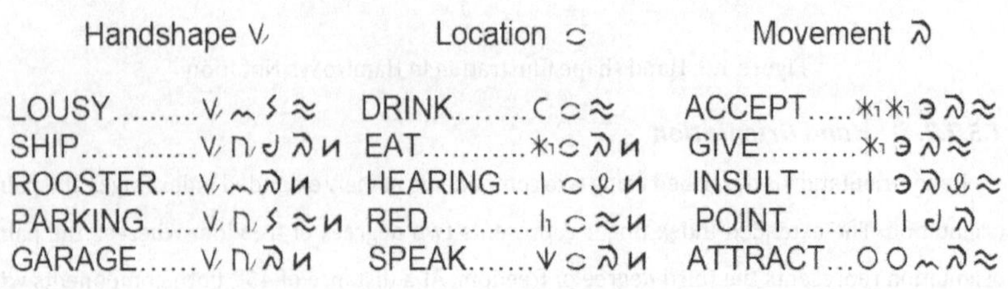

Figure 1.7: Example of ASL-Phabet Writing System

Unlike Stokoe notation, in ASL-Phabet there is an additional parameter added with the movement that is the contacting region of the hands. The sign writing is read from right to left in contrast with Stokoe notation constituting of four phonological parameters with the order of the first one as hand shape (H), the second location (L) and the third and fourth movement (M) or HLM which serves as the base for writing many words in ASL. Figure 1.7 (Supalla et al. 2014) shows the sample HLM representation in ASL-Phabet writing system.

1.5.4. SignWriting

SignWriting, a phonetic writing system, designed in 1974 by Dancer Valerie Sutton, is considered feature rich and 'visually iconic'; it includes mouthing, facial expression and dynamics of movement. It is mainly used for detailed research, language documentation and work publication in sign languages. SignWriting is designed to write in any language by using a number of symbols, including symbols for writing non-manual movements. The grapheme of the SignWriting includes hand shapes, orientation, body locations, facial expressions, contact and dynamic movements. Figure 1.8 (Hopkins 2008) represents ASL alphabetic representation in SignWriting.

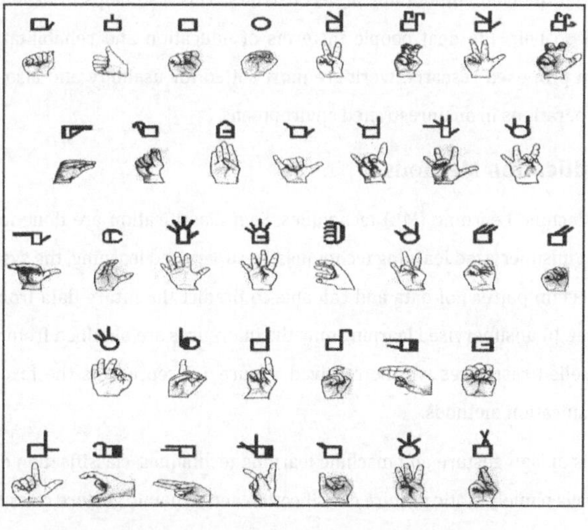

Figure 1.8: Alphabetic Representations in SignWriting

1.6. Applications of Sign Language Recognition

The most important applications of the proposed SLR are conversion of a sign language to text or speech. The development of automatic SLR system will improve the communication between the deaf and hard of hearing with the normal people. This research work aims in developing ASLRC to provide transcription system of sign languages to translate the signs to text and acts as an interface to support the integration of the deaf and hard of hearing with normal society. The proposed research work provides an interface with the help of laptop equipped with single web camera and the system does not require any external interfaces like sensors or coloured gloves. Using web camera, the system visually reads the signer actions of manual and non-manual signals and translates the performed signs into text.

SLR systems have a wide range of applications which includes HMI on ubiquitous computing, interfaces in public cubicles, translation and dialog interface systems for communication among people and sign synthesis systems. Sign synthesis systems incorporated with SLR systems can transfer the data where the sign is captured and detected at one end and translated using an avatar at the other end. Both the SLR and sign synthesis systems are used in sign language education.

Besides all these, the hard-of-hearing people can also have innate access to their social networks. In online applications, developing ASLRC helps the impaired people to access information from the web without any access barriers. This also helps in developing the sign language tutor to help the deaf people in terms of education and rehabilitation. All these applications on proposed research work are most suited for usability and also allows signer independent operations in an unrestricted environment.

1.7. Classification Methods

Based on Machine Learning (ML) techniques, Sign Classification are done in two ways as supervised and unsupervised learning techniques. In supervised learning, the system is trained to recognize certain pattern of data and can able to predict the future data from the labelled training data set. In unsupervised learning only the inferences are obtained from the input data set and no labelled responses will be received. Figure 1.9 represents the taxonomy of Sign Language Classification methods.

On the basis of sign gesture and machine learning techniques, classification of signs can be done in two ways namely static gesture classification and dynamic gesture classification. Static gesture classification involves in classifying the signs of static postures or single words without any time frames involved. This type of classification is used in case of recognizing isolated signs of the alphabet and numbers or finger-spelled words. Dynamic gesture classification is widely useful when there is a need to classify sequence of time frame with adjacent signs. This classification is generally used in recognizing continuous sign sentences.

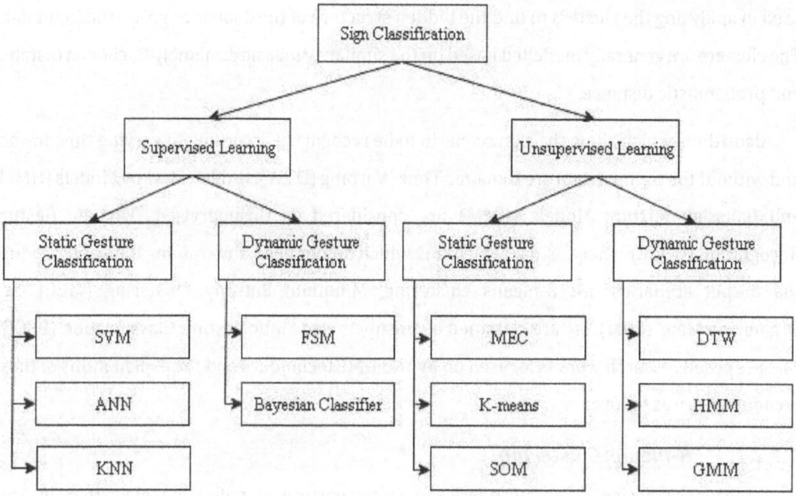

Figure 1.9: Classification of Sign Language Recognition based on Machine Learning Techniques

1.7.1. Supervised Machine Learning Techniques

Supervised learning techniques are used for predicting or inferring a sign function from the labelled training data. The training data is the one which consists of sign examples for training. A piece of example in supervised learning consists of the input data and its expected output value; that the learning algorithms analyzes the training data and produces the output as inferred function from labelled training data which can be used in mapping new training examples. Certain supervised learning algorithms should allow for the scenario to produce the labelled output even for the unseen sign instances.

According to static and dynamic varying sign gestures, classification can be done as static gesture classification and dynamic gesture classification. Algorithms which does not recognize with the varying time frames includes Support Vector Machine (SVM), Artificial Neural Networks (ANN), K-Nearest Neighbor (KNN), etc are classified as Supervised-Static Gesture Classification (SSGC) where as the algorithms that predict the inferred function from the training labelled data in varying time signals includes Bayesian Classifier and Finite State Machines (FSM) used for classifications are considered as Supervised Dynamic Gesture Classification (SDGC).

1.7.2. Unsupervised Machine Learning Techniques

Unsupervised machine learning is the task of inferring a function from the datasets consisting of input objects with unlabelled responses. Unsupervised learning is most commonly used in analyzing the clusters to find the hidden structure of the data or to group the input data. The clusters are generally modelled based on the similarity measures namely Euclidean distance and probabilistic distance.

Algorithms which allow the sign scenario to be recognized according to varying time frames and without the training data are Dynamic Time Warping (DTW), Hidden Markov Models (HMM) and Gaussian Mixture Models (GMM) are considered as Unsupervised Dynamic Gesture Recognition (UDGC) where as the algorithms which do not need any training data and produce the output scenarios are K-means clustering, Minimum Entropy Clustering (MEC), Self Organizing Maps (SOM), etc are classified as Unsupervised Static Gesture Classification (USGC). The proposed research work is focused on hybrid UML techniques and the explanations of these techniques are as follows:

1.7.2.1. K-means Clustering

K-means clustering is an unsupervised static gesture classification algorithm in Sign Language Recognition. K-means clustering is used to classify or to cluster the input data based on attributes into K number of clusters where K is the positive integer. K-means Clustering is the vector quantization approach which divides N observations into K clusters whereas the observation of each sign belongs to the cluster of the nearest mean. It is used in clustering the training data features of sign language into classes. General description of k-means clustering (Kriegel et al. 2016) is defined as given a set of observations ($x_1, x_2, ..., x_n$), where each observation is a d-dimensional real vector, k-means clustering aims to partition the n observations into k clusters where k should be less than or equal to n observations and sets S = {$S_1, S_2, ..., S_k$}.

$$\arg\min_{S} \sum_{i=1}^{k} \sum_{x \in S_i} \| x - \mu_i \|^2 = \arg\min_{S} \sum_{i=1}^{k} | S_i | Var S_i \qquad (1.1)$$

where μ_i is the mean of points in S_i.

This is equivalent to minimizing the pairwise squared deviations of points in the same cluster:

$$\arg\min_{S} \sum_{i=1}^{k} \frac{1}{2|S_i|} \sum_{x,y \in S_i} \| x - y \|^2 \qquad (1.2)$$

The Equivalence can be deduced from identity and it is calculated as

$$\sum_{x \in S_i} \| x - \mu_i \|^2 = \sum_{x \neq y \in S_i} (x - \mu_i)(\mu_i - y) \qquad (1.3)$$

1.7.2.2. *Hidden Markov Models*

HMM is a stochastic method for analyzing spatiotemporal variability of sign languages. HMM is used to recognize the time varying features of given signs based on the properties of Markov chains with two assumptions:

- The probability of a state depends only on the previous state.
- The probability of the output observation depends only on the state that results in the observation state and not with any other state.

A basic HMM deals with three fundamental problems: maximum likelihood of observation, decoding the probability of best hidden state sequence, and learning the HMM parameters.

- **Evaluating Likelihood:** For a particular hidden state sequence $Q = \{q_0, q_1, q_2, \ldots, q_T\}$ and an observation state sequence $O = \{o_1, o_2, \ldots, o_T\}$, the likelihood of the observation sequence is

$$P(O|Q) = \prod_{i=1}^{T} P(o_i \mid q_i) \tag{1.4}$$

- **Decoding:** Given as input an HMM, λ = (A,B) and a sequence of observations $O = \{o_1, o_2, \ldots, o_T\}$, the most probable sequence of states $Q = \{q_0, q_1, q_2, \ldots, q_T\}$ based on Viterbi algorithm (Jurafsky & Martin 2014) is

$$v_t(j) = \max_{i=1}^{N} v_{t-1}(i) a_{ij} b_i(o_t) \tag{1.5}$$

Where $v_{t-1}(i)$ the previous path probability from the previous time step, a_{ij} is the transition probability from previous state q_i to current state q_j and $b_j(o_t)$ is the state observation likelihood of the observation symbol o_t given the current state j.

- **Training:** Given an observation sequence O and the set of possible states in the HMM, the probability ξ_t is defined as the probability of being in state i at time t and state j at time t +1.

$$\xi(i, j) = P(q_t = i, q_{t+1} = j \mid O, \lambda) \tag{1.6}$$

and $$P(O \mid \lambda) = \alpha_T(q_F) = \beta_T(q_o) = \sum_{j=1}^{N} \alpha_t(j) \beta_t(j) \tag{1.7}$$

Where α and β are the forward and backward learning parameter with respect to forward state q_F and initial state q_o.

1.7.2.3. *Dynamic Time Warping*

Dynamic Time Warping is one of the algorithms used in time-series analysis to compute the similarity between two temporal sequences irrespective of the speed, velocity and frequency. For an instance in SLR, one signer may perform the signs faster than the other or there may be accelerations and decelerations of hands during the sign observation can be analyzed using DTW techniques. In general, DTW calculates the best matching with the optimal distance between two time series under certain restrictions that includes Boundary condition, Step Size Condition, Monotonicity condition, warping window condition and slope constraint condition.

Reyes et al. (2011) To find the best mapping between two temporal sequences A and B, one needs to find the path through the grid P = {p_1, ..., p_s , ..., p_k} where $p_s = (i_s , j_s)$ which minimizes the total distance between them, $p_k = (i_k, j_k) \in [1:I]\times[1:J]$ for $k \in [1:K]$ and P is called a warping function. Time-normalized distance between A and B is calculated as:

$$D(A,B) = \left[\frac{\sum_{s=1}^{k} d(p_s)\cdot w_s}{\sum_{s=1}^{k} w_s} \right] \tag{1.8}$$

Where $d(p_s)$ is the distance between i_s and j_s and $w_s > 0$ is the weighting coefficient. Best warping path P_0 between A and B is estimated as:

$$P_0 = \underset{P}{\arg\min}(D(A,B)) \tag{1.9}$$

Seeking a weighting coefficient function between the temporal sequences which guarantees that $C = \sum_{s=1}^{k} w_s$ is independent of the warping function. Thus the minimum distance between A and B is calculated as

$$D(A,B) = \frac{1}{C}\min_{P}\left[\sum_{s=1}^{k} d(p_s)\cdot w_s \right] \tag{1.10}$$

1.7.2.4. *Minimum Entropy Clustering*

Minimum Entropy Clustering is the unsupervised learning technique carried out by optimizing the overlap between the cluster densities. The MEC problem consists of two sub-problems namely estimating a posteriori probabilities of clusters and (ii) minimizing the overlap entropy. The Minimum Entropy clustering problem is formally stated as: Given a set of data X =

$\{x_i \mid i = 1, \ldots, n\}$ and an integer $m > 1$, map X onto $C = \{c_j \mid j = 1, \ldots, m\}$ so that every data x_i is assigned to at least one cluster c_j, the probability density function of one data is defined as

$$p(x) = \sum_{i=1}^{C} p(x \mid i) p(i) \tag{1.11}$$

Where p(i) is the prior probability of ith cluster. Shannon's entropy of a random variable X with a probability mass function p(x) is calculated as

$$H(X) = -\sum_{x} p(x) \log p(x) \tag{1.12}$$

Where H(x) is the random functional distribution of X, and it depends only on the probabilities of dataset X and not on its actual values. Based on Shanon's entropy (expected posteriori probability) and negative prior probability, the total measure of overlap Θ by Bayes Theorem is calculated as

$$\theta = -\sum_{i=1}^{k} p(i) \int p(x \mid i)[\log p(x \mid i) - \log p(x)] dx \tag{1.13}$$

Equation 1.13 is replaced with Shanon's entropy and the minimum entropy clustering criterion with posteriori probability is obtained as

$$\theta = -\left[H(X) - \sum_{i=1}^{k} p(i) H(X \mid i) \right] \tag{1.14}$$

1.8. Sign Language Recognition Approach

Recognition of sign languages can be achieved using vision-based approaches or sensor-based approaches. Vision-based systems can acquire the data using camera (single or stereo), active techniques (kinect or Leap Motion Controller) or invasive techniques (Coloured or data gloves, wrist bands and LED visions). Sensor-based systems acquire the sign information using instruments which includes Inertial Measurement Unit (IMU), Electromyography (EMG), Accelerometers and other electromagnetic sensors to capture the motion, position and the velocity of the hands.

Vision-based and sensor-based approaches differ mainly in the data acquisition stage. In the vision-based approach, static postures are acquired as images and for dynamic gestures the data is acquired as continuous frames of images. The data acquisition is done using web camera, single camera or multiple cameras. Sensor-based approaches use sensors, colour glove or data glove to acquire data from the users. In this approach, the users always require to wear a pair of coloured gloves on the arms of the signers.

Sign languages are composed of manual and non-manual components which constitute both spatial and temporal elements. Sign Language Recognition system focusing on static postures can recognize only small set of vocabularies. Hence, to recognize the large vocabulary sign gestures, certain methods are developed to incorporate the temporal characteristics of sign aspects. Such inherent model includes Neural Networks (NN), HMMs, FSMs, Bayesian Network and Template Matching Algorithm (TMA).

Vision-Based SLR systems started around mid 90's and focused on recognizing small vocabulary in the range of 40 to 50 signs. These systems were capable of recognizing static and dynamic signs under certain restrictions like using long sleeves, full collared neck and homogeneous background. The scalability problem arises because of these restrictions and limited vocabulary recognition. To address these issues, vision-based approach is enhanced in identifying the phonemes or chremes of the signs rather than classifying the whole signs. Such chreme based sign recognition is termed as Subunit-based SLR system. With the development of Subunit-based SLR, the recognition of large vocabulary is achieved to a certain degree with the limited training set.

In SLR, there are three types of new instances for any sign namely (i) signing of signer videos in training set, (ii) signing of the new signer and (iii) signs of different signers in training set. The signing of the signer in the training data set is called as signer dependent recognition, the signing of the new signer is called as signer independent recognition and the evaluation of similar signs of different signers and different signs of same signers in training set is called as cross-validation.

1.8.1. Recognition of Sign Level Gestures

Recognition of whole sign gestures involves recognizing signs performed by one hand or two hands. In single-handed signs, the signs are performed by only one hand and the hand performing the sign is said to be dominant hand. A sign in sign language usually represents the whole word; it is either a movement of the dominant hand or both the hands. However, in sign language, most of the special words such as name of a person are spelled out using static postures as the letters of the alphabet. One aspect of sign recognition involves recognizing static signs i.e. postures and the other aspect is recognizing dynamic signs i.e. gestures. The former is easier to recognize whereas the latter is highly complicated due to the varying time signals. Moreover, the SLR can be confronted as two types: Isolated Sign Recognition and Continuous Sign Recognition. Figure 1.10 represents the architecture of whole sign recognition system.

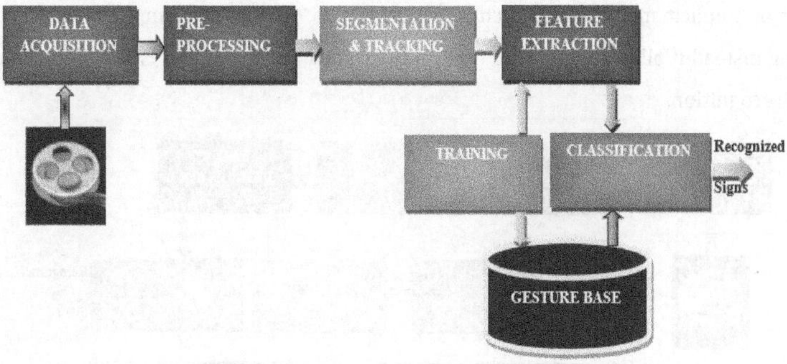

Figure 1.10: Architecture of Whole Sign Level Recognition System

1.8.1.1. *Isolated Sign Recognition*

Isolated signs are the sign gestures consisting of individual words, letters of the alphabet or numbers without any signs before or after the performed signs. Isolated Sign Recognition involves recognizing the signs performed individually that do not contain any preceding or succeeding signs. The research on ISR emphasises the importance of finding the best mathematical models and features for representing the signs. The HMM based approaches are well known to handle the temporal information of the signs by modelling different channels for different parameters. For a test sign, the model with the maximum likelihood is selected as the best path and the test sign is recognized as the sign of that model. The challenge arises in integrating both the hands in HMM model and to choose the best model to find the performed sign.

1.8.1.2. *Continuous Sign Recognition*

Continuous Sign Recognition attempts to recognize the entire stream of signs without any clear-cut pause or a marked boundary between the adjacent signs. In this perspective, CSR means that the signs within the continuous sentences are not separated by a pause. All the sentences with grammatically structured and meaningfully formed are considered as continuous sentences. Moreover, there is no restriction in forming a sentence structure. In CSR, the signs performed are affected by preceding and succeeding signs. The challenge arises in identifying the additional movements between the adjacent signs i.e. the formation of additional shapes or movements occurs during the transition from one to other. These transition movements are named as Epentheses Movements.

The EM problem is generally solved with implicit or explicit modelling of transition movements in continuous signing whereas the proposed research work does not involve an explicit or implicit modelling of such movements due to time consumption during manual labelling instead it allows the EMs to exist in the signed sentences and is pruned dynamically during recognition.

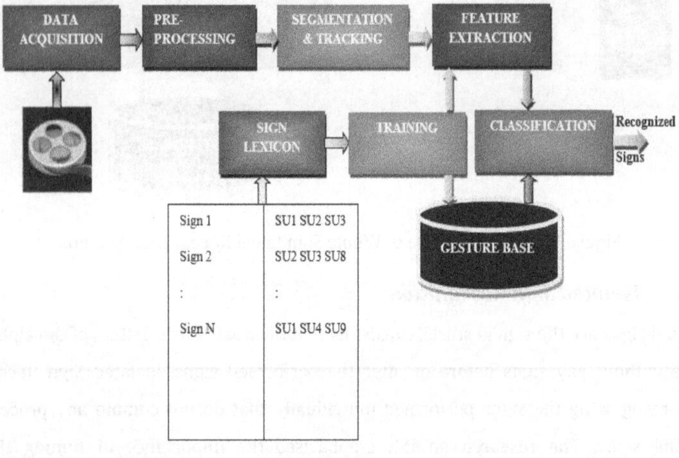

Figure 1.11: Architecture of Subunit Level Recognition System

1.8.2. Recognition of Subunit Level Sign Gestures

In SLR, it is not described which part of the sign serves as a good model for underlying subunit recognition. Most of the SLR systems are word based model where one word represents one sign in the gesture base. However, this whole sign recognition leads to certain drawbacks that are increase of complexity in training when the size of the vocabulary grows and the enhancement of vocabulary will also be problematic because the new sign is introduced in the context of other sign in training.

Subunits are the small segments of subdivisions of signs which can either be linguistically derived using phonemes or visually derived using the feature cues. The number of subunits for individual sign can be chosen in such a way that the sign is modelled. Modelling of signs as concatenation of sub-units as in the modeling of phonemes in speech recognition will be more beneficial than the modeling of signs as whole words.

Figure 1.11 illustrates the subunit segmentation based on spatiotemporal cues and its similarity in sharing the clusters. The merits of proposed subunit level sign recognition include:

- The amount of training data set that will be reduced since each sign consists of a limited number of subunits.

- The further enhancement of the vocabulary of signs that can be achieved from the existing subunits for the new signs.
- The gesture space and time consumption for the subunit construction can be reduced due to sharing of two or more subunits among different signs.
- The general vocabulary size can be increased.

1.8.2.1. Linguistic-Oriented Subunit Representation

In speech recognition, subunits are considered from syllable, half-syllables or phonemes. The basic nature of the subunits is derived in accordant with orthography that is the standard notation available for subunit representation in speech recognition. While transferring the same aspect in SLR, the linguistic breakdown of signs is not yet standardized and there are various notations available for such subunit representation. But unfortunately, there is no equally acceptable notation system subsists for SLR. The most acceptable subunit notations are Stokoe's notation and Liddell and Johnson's Movement-Hold notation.

Stokoe's Notation (Stokoe 1991) was the first available subunit notation in linguistic-oriented SLR. Corresponding to the term phonemes, the term chremes was introduced by Stokoe to represent the subunits in sign languages. The employed chremes are accepted as subunits but the practical implementation of such linguistic subunits are still challenging. Stokoe's chremes are performed in parallel whereas in SLR, the signs are performed in subsequent order. Also, it has many entities of signs but the notations are not available for all the signs. Even though Stokoe's notation is considered as good system for linguistic breakdown of signs, the system will not use a base for SLR without manual alterations.

Liddell & Johnson (1989) introduced another chreme based notation based on the two parameters: Movements and Holds. Movement chreme represents the sign moves and holds represents the configuration of the hands. Stokoe's notations are performed in parallel whereas the movement and hold model consider the subunits in sequential manner. Similar to stokoe, there is no comprehensive lexicon available in movement-hold notation for all sign entities. Furthermore, the detailed coding for the video-based articulatory features will cause additional problems and it is not possible to achieve such high level detail with this notation.

1.8.2.2. Visual-Oriented Subunit Representation

The visual-oriented notation for SLR does not need any prior linguistic knowledge about the signs. The segmentation of signs into subunits is based on the data-driven approach, that is, the subunits are formed from the data itself without any prior knowledge on source. Here, the sign breakdown begins with different segments without any semantic meaning and the subsequent process will determine the similarities among the segments. Segments with similar features are then pooled together and labelled and considered as on subunit. Now, each sign can have more than one subunit with the distinguished labels. Figure 1.12 shows the example "JOHN READ BOOK" from RWTH-BOSTON-104 data set to illustrate the subunit division based on visual descriptors.

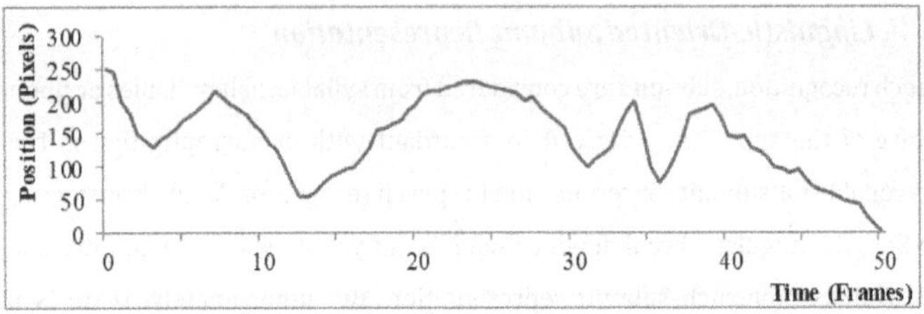

Figure 1.12: Possible Subunit Segmentation for the Sentence "JOHN READ BOOK" from RWTH-BOSTON-104

1.9. Contribution of the Book

This book Subunit Sign Modelling for Continuous Sign Language concentrates on ASLRC and examines the Vision-Based SLR system including isolated sign recognition and continuous sign language recognition. Also, this proposed work concentrates on recognizing large-vocabularies of sign languages without an intuitive or interface devices. The developed Subunit Level Sign Language Recognition System improves scalability, portability, usability and user-friendliness.

- The first contribution aims at solving the two important issues (1) Subunit feature extraction and (2) Signer independent action on visual sign language recognition. Subunit extraction is involved in the sequential and parallel breakdown of sign gestures without any prior knowledge on syllables and number of subunits. A novel Bayesian Parallel Hidden Markov Model (BPaHMM) is introduced for subunit extraction to combine the features of manual and non-manual parameters to yield better results in classification and recognition of signs. Signer independent action aims in using a single web camera for different signer behaviour patterns and for cross-signer validation.
- The second contribution of the book is addressing the problem of hand segmentation ambiguities and segregating epentheses movements between two adjacent signs in continuous video sequences. A novel subunit sign modelling framework is presented and illustrated to embark upon these problems while considering large-vocabularies. This framework is developed using a novel methodology of Enhanced Dynamic Programming (EDP) approach in subunit sign modelling. This EDP framework works with a

combination of dynamic time warping and spatiotemporal clustering techniques. The distance is used as a temporal feature vector and clustered with spatial feature vectors using Minimum Entropy Clustering. This process is done recursively to cluster all the epentheses movements dynamically without using any explicit or implicit modelling.

- The third contribution of this proposed research work is constructing the subunit sign modelling framework for automatic sign language recognition. This contribution involves in modelling Spatial/Temporal subunits, construction of subunits, construction of subunit Sign Lexicon and training and recognition of subunits. The proposed work introduces Subunit Multi-stream Parallel HMM (SMP-HMM) to model these components and develops the novel Subunit Sign Modelling framework for Continuous Sign Language Recognition.

1.10. Organization of the Book

The structure of the reminder of the book has been organized as variously as follows: Chapter 2 presents the various techniques in the state-of-the art of sign language recognition and the major unsolved issues in sign language recognition. Chapter 3 illustrates the architecture of proposed subunit sign modelling framework and Chapter 4 to chapter 6 discusses the major contributions of the proposed research work. The implemented idea of extricating the subunit level manual and non-manual components of continuous signs using vision-based sign recognition systems is detailed in Chapter 4. In addition to this, the evaluation has been done on important feature selection, combinations of different feature cues and signer independent validation.

Chapter 5 elaborates the technique of using Enhanced Dynamic Programming approach in handling the epentheses movements and hand segmentation ambiguities from continuous signing sentences. Experimental evaluation has been done in analyzing and segmenting the epentheses movements.

Chapter 6 presents a novel framework for subunit modelling for continuous sign language recognition. It discusses the various aspects on integrating Spatial/Temporal subunits and constructing sign lexicon. Experimental results are analyzed and discussed with respect to phonetic based SU construction and construction; Continuous Sign Sentences are evaluated against RWTH-PHOENIX-Weather data set and isolated signs are evaluated against ASLLVD data set and also the evaluation has been done for whole sign modelling versus subunit sign modelling.

Although each chapter has a separate concluding section, Chapter 7 presents an overall concluding remarks of the contributions and possible future directions of this research work.

CHAPTER II

2. Literature Review

2.1. Introduction

Research in the field of automatic sign language recognition has made momentous progression over the last few years. This chapter deals with the review on the state of the art literature on sign language recognition and classification and highlight the issues faced by the present recognition system for which the proposed research work intends the solutions. The research done by various authors are also studied and some of the important papers are discussed in this chapter.

The present state of the art on SLR is approximately 30 years behind speech recognition systems owing manifold causes. One of the primary reasons behind this is processing and recognizing the two-dimensional video signals are highly complex than processing the one-dimensional audio signals. Besides, sign language lexical and semantic items are not yet fully discovered, and also, no standard dictionaries exist. Apart from these, for such large number of signs no common definitions exist. Sign language recognition and classification has reaches its perseverance of research publications in the beginnings of 90's. Mostly, the presented system takes almost of 10 seconds to process the signer's video and translate to text.

The data acquisition methods plays vital role in classifying the primary features of different works on SLR. Many researchers have used data gloves or cyber gloves to extract the features of the manual and non-manual components of the signs because of the reliability of the sensor-based SLR systems. However, for the signer, the use of such sensors are quiet unnatural and more restrictive. Also, the practical implementations of sensor-based SLR systems are infeasible due to the expensive nature of sensors.

On the other hand, vision-based SLR systems have greatly influenced the researchers by their heftiness and their ability to handle cluttered, dynamic inhomogeneous environments and variations under different illuminations and occlusions in the feature extraction stage. Many of the publications have not addressed these issues explicitly; instead they suggest that the system works well in homogeneous background with a common constraint that the signer needs to wear long-sleeved clothes that differs from the skin tone of the signers allowing colour detection method to detect face and hands of the signer.

The common part of the SLR systems supports indirectly the signer dependent operations i.e. all the signers are trained before using the SLR system. In turn, signer-independent or cross-validation among the signers involves in normalization of features to remove the dependencies of signers. The constraints that include the distance between the signer and the camera, position of the signer and the resolution of the camera are rarely published.

The earlier stages of SLR focused on isolated signs similar to speech recognition. Even though several SLR systems have been developed for recognizing continuous sentences, the recognition rate reached up to 90% only for small vocabularies. In continuous sign sentences, the epentheses movement exists in between the adjacent signs. The past researches do not specifically mentioned whether these are modelled explicitly, implicitly or simply ignored. If the transition movements also modelled along with the signs, the gesture base will be increased. Unless it is modelled or ignored, the transition movements may be wrongly classified as sign.

Based on state-of-the-art on sign language recognition, the current recognition system recognizes a large vocabulary only by using sensor-based devices. Many of the systems are signer-dependent, and the recognition rates are valid for the restricted test scenario. Information about heftiness on real-time applications of the SLR systems is not available widely. Moreover, the exact collections of the vocabularies are not known and there is no standard dictionary available for such vocabularies. In summary, none of the present recognition systems in the literature meets the strong real-life application requirements.

2.2. Data Acquisition and Sign Tracking

The first step in sign recognition is data acquisition and tracking of sign gestures. The data is acquired in the form of frames of images for the continuous video sequences. Once the data is acquired, the pre-processing of all such images will begin to modify the given video sequences to improve the performance of the SLR systems. In pre-processing, Median filter, Gaussian filter and morphological filters are the most commonly used for noise reduction.

2.2.1. Sign Gesture Pre-Processing

Median filtering operation was used by Rao et al. (2006) to sort the pixel values of the window in ascending order and chooses the middle value. The median filter is implemented by using the sliding window concept in an image. A 3X3 window has been chosen to process the image and considered as effective for all the image sizes. Yu et al. (2010) used median filter to remove the impulse noises from the acquired manual features and to preserve the sharp edges of the hands. After that, they used smoothing filter to reduce the neighbourhood radius and detain the good quality of the hand shapes.

A 2D Gabor filter and Gaussian filter were used by Pugeault & Bowden (2011) to extract the hand shape and to remove the noise in the frames. Gabor filter collects the features based on the intensity of the depth images and Gaussian Filter is used in the range of 128 X 128 images to obtain the envelope on the Gaussian basis of 8 X 8 grid. Agarwal & Thakur (2013) generated the feature matrix from the stream of depth images using the collective stream information and applied a Gaussian blur filter to squelch the noise and generate a clear depth map for the single stream of video inputs. The parameters were hand tuned for both blurring and squelching operations in their experiments.

A morphological closing operator was used by Habili et al. (2004) to fill the holes in the segmented images. In addition to the holes, bright spots and shadows are also removed from the frames using morphological closing operator. Morphological closing operator fills the small and thin holes, smoothens the boundaries of the regions without affecting the geographical area. Admasu & Rajmond (2010) used morphological opening operations namely erosion and dilation to estimate the background illumination and to obtain the uniformity the illuminated image was subtracted from the original image. In addition to this, median filter is used to reduce the impulsive noise from the image.

2.2.2. *Sign Gesture Segmentation*

Skin colour segmentation and tracking of the sign gesture is feasible in SL recognition due to the illumination and variation of skin colour from the background objects. Even though the distribution is not uniform, skin segmentation will be highly beneficial while segmenting the faces from the video sequences. Skin colour segmentation using chrominance component is performed by Chai & Ngan (1999). They suggested two reasons for using the chrominance component. The first reason is, skin-colour segmentation algorithm will be invariant to the changes in brightness. The second reason is that there must be the difference in skin colour among different races of people that are categorized by the brightness of the skin colour.

The range of the skin colour for the face and hands from the HSV colour space was determined by Taniba et al. (2002). When the face and hands are overlapped, the texture template is obtained from the face and hand shapes of the previous frames. Habili et al. (2004) implemented YCbCr colour space in their research for the effective modelling of algorithm. The authors have stored and coded the video in YCbCr colour space. Since conversion is expensive and requires more time, this research work does not concentrate on converting from one space model to another.

A segmentation method based on Gaussian model was introduced by Bergasa et al. (2000) to overcome the challenges in skin colour spaces. The authors made different comparative studies and concluded that the normalized RGB space model provides accurate results in complex backgrounds. Holden et al. (2005) detected the skin colour components using Principal Component Analysis (PCA) of the RGB colour space. Their method identifies the detected skin objects using the shapes and locations of the hands and face in the image sequence.

The colour of the markers in HSV colour spaces using motion detection techniques was estimated by Keskin & Akarun (2009). The obtained features are extracted and smoothened using kalman filter to form the 2D trajectories of the hand motion. Similarly Han et.al (2009) & Han et al. (2013) also used kalman filter to track the sign gesture obtained using Support Vector Machine learning and region segmentation. But these trackers are non-robust in cluttered environments and for the signer's wearing short sleeves. Nonetheless, the above methods discussed does not describe the recognition of continuous natural signing and it still remains challenging in terms of video-based analysis due to the multimodal fusion nature of SLR systems are lip movements, facial expressions and body poses.

2.2.2.1. *Sensor-Based Approaches*

Researchers have used various sensor-based approach to capture sign gestures are data gloves (Assaleh et al. 2012, Shukor et al. 2015), power gloves (Mohandes et al. 2004), digital camera (Hongo et al. 2000), accelerometer (Zhang et al. 2011), depth camera (Almeida et al. 2014), Kinect (Lai et al. 2012), Leap motion controller (Chuan et al. 2014) or dexterous master gloves (Hoshino 2006).

A smart glove was designed (Sadek et al. 2017) to analyze the anatomical shape of the hands using fewer sensors based on the statistical methods for recognizing Arabic Sign Language. The glove costs around 65 dollars where the authors claim that the designed glove costs lesser than 5 percent of the commercially available gloves. However, the usage of such gloves is expensive and also, the recognition needs the coloured markers or vision based techniques to classify the signs. The coloured gloves or coloured markers (Wang & Popovic 2009, Elbendary et al. 2010) are placed on the wrist or fingertips on the signer respectively. These pretended colours from the frames are detected and segmented to identify the sign gesture using image processing techniques. Conversely, the signers will lack the natural way of signing by constantly wearing these gloves.

The introduction of low cost sensors like kinect and leap motion controller is highly useful in collecting the 3D data more conveniently. Kinect sensor comes along with the Software

Development Kit and its openNI library to recognize the skeleton of entire body. So it is infeasible to recognize the crucial features of sign language that includes fingertip and lip movements. The Kinect sensor was used by Raheja et al. (2011) to locate the fingertips and palm in their research. The authors have produced an accuracy of nearly 90% in detecting the features. However, they have not developed the application for sign gesture recognition. Similar approaches (Wen et al. 2012, Suarez & Murphy 2012) to recognize fingertip and palm orientations using hand contour and convex hull from the segmented hand is discussed. Despite effective results, unfortunately both the approaches lead the recognition of small gestures problem unsolved in terms of occlusions.

On the other hand, Rossol et al. 2016 used Leap Motion controller (LMC) to obtain 3D data with millimetre level accuracy for the sampling rate 120 frames per second. This device has been specially designed for recognizing hand and finger gestures and to extract features namely fingertip points, palm orientation and palm location. Before LMC was used for recognizing hand gestures, it had been used widely in various other applications. Cho & Lee et al. (2014) introduced LMC in honeybee series gaming for kids using hand gestures.

Vamsikrishna et al. (2016) used LMC for palm and finger spine rehabilitation by interfacing with the computing device to record the features to describe 3D movements which involves in rehabilitation and in upper limb rehabilitation (Charles et al. 2013). Also this device has been used in human computer interaction (Palacios et al. 2013) and stroke rehabilitation (Kadhemi et al. 2014). Even though it has many applications, this device has only a small field of view when compared with kinect. Therefore, the usage of LMC has been restricted to obtain only hand and finger movements.

2.2.2.2. *Vision-Based Approaches*

Computer vision-based techniques on the other hand use bare hands without any coloured gloves or sensors. Compared to sensor-based approaches, vision-based techniques are considered to have high mobility and normality for the signers and also, cost effective due to the usage of single camera. There are a few works which rely on acquiring 2D using single camera in SLR. For all these merits, vision-based approaches suffered in changing illuminations and when occlusions (hand to hand or face to hand) occur due to the lack of depth information features in 2D images. In the vision-based approach, either skin colour detection or background subtraction will be used to segment the sign gestures.

A skin detection method was used by Kawulok (2008) where the eyes and mouth in the face region are included to consider as the non-skin regions and calculated the probability of the pixel value to estimate skin and non-skin pixels. In turn, their approach itself affects the results due to the misclassification of mouth, eyes and eyebrows pixels as skin tone which is actually not true. Another approach (Bilal et al. 2015) used the skin tone pixels in the center of 10 X 10 window of face region. In most of the researches, it is considered as the nose tip of the face region. This approach could not cope with the illumination variations and it lead to wrong indications of skin pixel identifications. Background removing technique followed by dynamic skin detector component based on face skin colour was designed by Ibrahim et al. (2012). The authors have applied the skin detection technique directly to the frames and the obtained difference is used to segment the hands from the frames from the video sequence. Furthermore, this technique can merely used when the hands are the only moving objects in the subsequent frames.

The trajectory estimation of a moving object in an image plane as tracking was designed by Yilmaz et al. (2006). There are several approaches has been proposed to track the moving objects using vision-based approaches. Some of them are: Active hand contour and convex modelling (Chen et al. 2003, Holden et al. 2005), skin blob based tracking (Sherrah & Gong 2000, Zaki & Shaheen 2011), camshift (Li et al. 2011, Huang & Hong 2011), Kalman filter (Zieren et al. 2002) and particle filter (Gianni et al. 2007).

The target of moving objects was detected by Salmond & Birch (2001) using particle filter. This approach lacks practicality and needs many calculative works before processing the images. Wang & Lin (2009) proposed an improvement strategy which aimed at reducing the computational complexity of the unscented particle filter algorithm. This strategy highly reduces the practical difficulties without any loss of accuracy but the speed of system is not still enough even after the improvement in particle filter algorithm.

To overcome these practical issues, Chu et al. (2007) introduced a Camshift algorithm to combine the differences in subsequent frames. This method has the advantage of overcoming artificial orientations and to move forward immediately. However, this technique still faces the problem of forward segmentation accuracy. Also it can track only moving objects and it will not predict objects in the frame without motions. To solve this limitation, improved Camshift algorithm (Li et al. 2011, Huang & Hong 2011) is used to detect the active motion of the object using camera. However, the accuracy of the systems still remains questionable.

Dynamic programming tracking (Dreuw et al. 2006) is developed to track the hands. In this technique, two tracking paths have been considered and relies the correct path to decide the hand objects. This dynamic programming tracking combines with cascade boosting technique to improve the overall score function for all the frames in a sequence (Ibrahim et al 2017) and 0% tracking error rate. However, the two-path tracking method requires lot of computations and the score function needs more modifications to obtain the required results.

In the proposed approach, hand and face localization and tracking are performed by identifying skin pixels in the area of interest using enhanced peer algorithm in HSV colour space. This algorithm is based on the colour detection and motion cues of the hand gestures. In the pre-processing stage, the static background is subtracted from the dynamic video sequence. Background subtraction involves two subsequent processes: Erosion and Dilation. The proposed approach does not have any imaging constraints and restrictions which includes uniform background, long full-sleeved clothing or required to wear any sensors or coloured markers to identify the skin pixels. Also, it does not involve in complex calculations in tracking the hand trajectories. Henceforth, the computation cost of the system remains constant and it does not affect the natural signing way of signers.

2.3. Feature Extraction and Parameter Estimation

Vision-based feature extraction approaches depend on the computer vision and image processing techniques for dealing with features which includes hand shape estimation, gesture segmentation, contour and boundary modelling, and colour and motion cue identification. Researches in the field of SL have to be understood whether the system has been designed to recognize continuous signs or isolated signs. In the former case, the upper body of the signer has to be considered for extracting the features whereas in the latter case only the finger orientation and configuration need to be considered. Hence, for developing the fully automatic SLR system, both the cases have to be formulated for extracting the manual and non-manual features.

2.3.1. Manual Feature Extraction

Manual gestures are the ones which consist of both spatial and temporal features are hand shape, position and motion. All these features are continuously changing and have different parameters and characteristics. All these parameters are modelled separately and considered as different modalities of features. The various hand shape modelling approaches are: Appearance-based modelling or 2D features modelling, 3D-based Modelling and variational segmentation modelling.

2.3.1.1. Appearance-Based Modelling

Appearance based modelling of sign gestures are used to extract the hand shape features from the projected intensity images and discovered to relate the extracted features with the actual shapes. Various hand appearance based feature parameters includes segmented hand moments, image Eigen vectors, hand contours and Scale Invariant Feature Transform (SIFT) moments, and binary hand silhouettes or manual hand blobs (Starner et al. 1998, Elmezian et al. 2008). Cui & weng (2000) introduced segmented hand moments to normalize the size, illumination and in-plane orientation. They have used Principal Component Analysis for dimensionality reduction of the features before processing the segmented moments (Deng & Tsui 2002).

The Eigen tracker algorithm was proposed by Gupta et al. (2002) to track the hand and changes in the hand shape to satisfy the purpose of associating semiotics to the gesture. However, Eigen tracking algorithm shows the inefficiency due to the absence of predictive framework. A hierarchical decision tree was formed by Coogan & Sutherland (2006) where the leaf nodes contain the hand shapes and they have used fuzzy k-means clustering to combine the obtained Eigen values from PCA of artificially trained shapes. Though the system works with gloves, the system is improbable to track under various illuminations.

Hand contour based approaches are involved in various translation, rotation, scale and invariant features namely Fourier descriptors (Huang & Huang 1998, Chen et al. 2003), curvature representors (Dominio et al. 2014, Marin et al. 2014), distance measures (Grzeszcuk et al. 2000), size functions (Bauer & Kraiss 2001) and localized hand contour formations (Gupta & Ma 2001, Bowden & Sarhadi 2002). Grzeszcuk et al. (2000) proposed a hybrid gesture representation approach to work under extreme lighting and to tolerate different hand postures. The authors have developed an algorithm using 2D distance metric to calculate the geometric features of hand poses. However, this system works well and produced effective results only for 6 trained gestures.

Hand shape using active contour shape model was proposed by Huang & Jeng (2001) and they have extracted the distance as Hausdroff measure of distance to calculate the size as distance between prestored image and the input image. Though the hand contour-based models use invariant feature representation, these models suffer from ambiguity which results from similar contours of different shapes. Roussos et al. (2010) extracted the hand shape features by employing Affine-invariant shape appearance model to offer a compact and discriminative feature version of hand configurations. Later, the hand shape features extracted via this model was integrated to form the subunits. However this system produced around 85% accuracy in subunit level for isolated signs.

Local Binary patterns similar to scale and translation invariant features are generated from edge depth image (Feris et al. 2004) and are used to achieve the high recognition performances. Notably, this approach has produced good recognition rates and it discriminates between similar signs. Zahedi et al. (2006) combined down-sampled original images and binary skin intensity images to obtain the down-sampled features by using sobel filters (Zahedi et al. 2005). A method for tracking entirely the volumetric Haar-like features in subunit level was proposed by Cooper et al. (2011). But, the variability of signers brings in the problem of temporal inconsistencies between adjacent signs.

Ibrahim et al. (2017) used hand blobs or binary silhouettes to identify and track the hands. Geometric features are formulated to form the feature vectors of the hand and produced 97% accuracy. But their system has been able to recognize only 30 isolated words and it does not work with continuous sign gestures. All these 2D-based modelling techniques are low cost due to the usage of single camera and require more computation time while recognizing the gestures under various illuminations. Also, when the occlusion occurs, these techniques really suffer in handling them under critical real-time environments.

2.3.1.2. 3D-Based Modelling

3D-based feature modelling is a more complex geometrical modelling which uses prior knowledge about the hand geometry. This paves the way to modelling the 3D-based features to represent the sign gestures and to overcome the shortcomings due to occlusions in signing. A 3D-model based approach (Dorner & Hagen 1994, Holden & Owens 2001) is used to estimate the finger joint angles and orientations of 3D hands. Cootes et al. (2000) used 3D based modelling to represent the hand contour with the restriction on the sort of joint angles and state transitions. The recognition system works under these constraints to successfully track the gestures in different rotations. However, the system requires 5 to 6 seconds to process the single frame.

The 3D model using coloured markers was projected by Holden & Owens (2001) and they removed the occlusions by using Kalman-filter prediction. Though the problem of hand occlusion was solved, the system has the constraint on hand orientation: the palm of the hand should always face the camera. Nolker & Ritter (2002) also used 3D hand models with the assumption that the area of interest within the frame should only possess the hand features with high resolution. But in the SLR, the region of interest will always contain the entire upper body and the resolution and size of the hands will be minimized which degrades the accuracy of SLR system. Also, this did not give the solution for hand occlusions.

A 3D hand shape model for matching the binary edges of cluttered images to edges formed from the hand shape model was used by Athitsos & Scarloff (2003). Each matching has been given a possible quantitative value from which the possible rank lists of hand shapes are obtained. However, their system works well under small angle of rotation and translation but it fails when major variations are introduced. Riviere & Guitton (2004) used 3D model based approaches in an attempt to minimize the shortcomings of the above approaches. They extracted feature difference between the pretended 3D model and the input image sequence directly with nine degrees of freedom for hands. Experimental results against uniform background yielded 10 percent of error and the system required furthermore work before the model could be applied in the real-time signing environment.

3D model-based hand tracking system was discussed by Stenger et al. (2006) to generate the contours and to compare the edges of the images. This model handles the occlusions using unscented Kalman filter. Generally, using filtering techniques requires more computation time. Hamada et al. (2004) used the similar approach for hand tracking to remove the occlusion and background clutters. However, both these methods require large amount of training data to build the accurate hand models. Razaei et al. (2008) proposed an algorithm for the estimation of the 3D motion trajectory from stereo camera and orientation of a hand using Fourier descriptors. The authors have resolved the problem of detecting the trajectories and orientation of signer's hand but they have made an assumption for the accurate match between the feature points and then they deal with 3D trajectory estimation.

3D depth camera was used by Hadfield & Bowden (2010) to segment the hands based on the naive assumption that the hands should always be close to the camera. But in the SLR, it is highly infeasible due to more number of variations in the signing space. Elons et al. (2014) generated 3D hand model for the hand postures and produce the single 3D feature from two 2D images. They have classified 50 Arabic Sign Language (ArSL) using hybrid pulse-couple neural network. However, the misclassification comes from the non-deterministic finite automata for some gestures while the new gestures included in finite sets.

More recently there are few frameworks which recognize multimodal gestures. Fok et al. (2015) used two leap motion controllers to recognize 3D finger movements for ASL. Kumar et al. (2017) used one leap motion controller and one Kinect sensor to capture finger and palm orientations. The LMC is kept below the hands of the signers whereas the Kinect sensor is placed in front of the signer focused on horizontal and vertical movements of the fingers of the hands. However, using the 3D-based modelling requires expensive devices and more computations even though these methods ignored pre-processing techniques. Also, both these methods affected the signer's natural way of signing and their frequency of signing. In addition to this, the recognition of multimodal recognition framework needs more computation due to the usage of multiple sensors.

To overcome the shortcomings of the existing feature extraction techniques namely occlusion in 2D-modelling and expensive modelling of 3D gestures, the proposed framework extracts the 3D Spatio-temporal features from video sequences and converts that to 2D images based on hand blob segmentation in the frames. Also, the proposed approach combines the spatial features (hand shape appearance based on the contour using Fourier descriptors) with the temporal features (motion trajectories) to get the accurate hand model in the sequence of frames. Since the features are extracted 3D sequences, the occlusion over the hands and face is easily removed. In addition to this the proposed approach does not require the users to wear 3D devices, so it will greatly support the practical implementation of real-time SLR system.

2.3.2. *Non-manual Feature Extrication*

In addition to the manual-cues, non-manual features are also extremely crucial and contain significant amount of information to recognize in sign gestures. The non-manual signals could be operated as indicators, semantic properties of the signs, or lexical, syntactical and grammatical functions which includes negation, clausal type, question status, and topics. The most important among the non-manual features are facial expressions (Tian et al. 2005), lip shapes and head pose (Murphy-Chutorian & Trivedi 2009). Fasel & Luettin (2003) made a survey on automatic analysis of facial expressions. However, their technique cannot be applied directly to the extract the facial expressions due to the inability to characterize temporal expressions and its limited robustness.

Apart from the linguistic preferences, the non-manual components have also been used as an aid to the recognition of manual components (Aran et al. 2007) and in some cases they have been used as an interpretation of grammatical markers (Metaxas et al. 2012). Many of the existing works focussing on interpreting the non-manual cues which involve in constructing the mapping functions between the low level features (Metaxas et al. 2012) and high level component features (Nguyen & Ranganath 2008). The non-manual feature extraction can be categorized as under, based on the two methodologies: classification-based method (Zhao & Zhang 2011) and action-based method. The former one involves identifying a small set of facial expressions related to mental activities and to identify the intensities of these expressions (Rudovic et al. 2012) whereas the later involves identifying the facial expressions related to actions of facial muscles and to relate those actions with respect to intensities and location (Valstar & Pantic 2012). However, the classification-based approaches collects the data in laboratory environments with constraints that frontal-view should face the camera and label the data with few occlusions. But these constraints cannot withstand in SLR due to data acquisition in more natural settings. Similarly, the action-based methodologies attempts to recognize the motion patterns relevant to linguistics and not to use that information as grammatical markers but these actions require prior modelling of all the linguistic information.

There are certain other issues with respect to non-manual components like head pose estimation and head nods and shakes. Head poses can be estimated using active appearance models (Cootes et. al 2001), shape models (Kanaujia et al. 2006) and constrained models (Cristinacce & Cootes 2006). Kelly et al. (2009) and Jian-zheng & Zheng (2011) made efforts to recognize head motions along with periodic movements. However, movement properties and differentiation of the temporal features for sub-classification of the sign gestures have not been considered in their works. In addition to facial expressions and head movements, Reale et al. (2011), Berreti et al. (2013) and Caridakis et al. (2014) also included lip movements but they discarded the manual information. To recognize the complete sign gestures, a fully automatic system requires the simultaneous aspects of both manual and non-manual features.

Recently some works have focused on combining the manual and non-manual feature parameters to recognize the sign gestures. Aran et al. (2009) combined the manual and non-manual parameters in a two-step process of SLR. In the first step, the manual features were extracted and in the second step, the non-manual features were extracted to resolve the ambiguity. However, their approach cannot be extended towards the recognition of real-time SLR system. Yang et al. (2013) proposed a method to combine manual and non-manual parameters. They have used hierarchical conditional random field to segment the manual features, boostmap to verify hand shapes and support vector machine to recognize non-manual parameters. However, they produced an accuracy of only 84% in recognizing gestures. Kumar et al. (2017) have combined manual and non-manual features using leap motion controller and kinect sensors to recognize sign gestures and produced an accuracy of accuracy of 96.01%. Nonetheless, this system will work only with the 3D-based devices which affect the signer's signing frequency.

2.4. Classification Methods

Based on the machine learning techniques, the classification techniques can be categorized as supervised and unsupervised learning. Based on these techniques, the SLR system can recognize the static and dynamic gestures of signs. There are several classification techniques existing for SLR. Some of the notable classification techniques include Neural Networks (NNs), Hidden Markov Models, Support Vector Machine (SVM), KNN, K-means Clustering, Self-Organizing Maps (SOM), Dynamic Time Warping, Finite State Machines, Kalman Filtering, Particle Filtering, Condensation Algorithm and Bayesian Classifier.

2.4.1. Neural Networks

The earliest classification work applied Neural Networks (NN) to recognize the static gestures of SLR. The first machine learning classification came into existence in the mid of 90's with the sensor devices. Murakami & Taguchi (1991) published their first research article on SL recognition approaches based on NNs. They trained the features obtained from the data gloves using NN and classified the isolated signs. Their system did not address the issues of extending the recognition to continuous signs. Another similar glove -based approach was introduced using Fuzzy Min-Max NN (Kim et al. 1996) with the help of data gloves to recognize 25 isolated signs with an accuracy of 85 %. A simple Vision-based SLR (Huang et al. 1995) was introduced to recognize the isolated signs using Hopfield NN. Time Delay Neural Network (TDNN) was introduced by Yang et al. (2002) to overcome the problem of motion segmentation and they proved that their system achieved encouraging results.

Gesture Recognition Fuzzy Neural Network (GRFNN) was introduced by Binh & Toshiaki (2005) to recognize isolated ASL words of large vocabulary. They used fuzzy control techniques to learn the parameters. However, their system had the advantage of increasing accuracy only when the training pattern was preselected. Akmeliawati et al. (2009) used ANN to recognize the hand gestures. They trained the system with 7392 gesture signals for 13 different gestures and achieved an accuracy of 96.02%. Despite its increasing accuracy, this system required more training samples and it could not be applied directly to the SLR.

To recognize the continuous data of Persian isolated signs by employing the Multi-layered Perceptron Neural Network (MLPNN) and distinguish the data which was not done by TDNN. Their system produced an accuracy of 94.06% but the speed of the system was quite slow. Zhang et al. (2011) introduced Annealing Back Propagation Neural Network (ABPNN) to recognize the hand gestures. This is the only technique which uses feed backward connection and remembers the past cues. Another NN technique is Recurrent Neural Network (RNN) (Barros et al. 2013) used Elman RNN to recognize 4 gestures. MLPNN is the feed forward NN and it is highly flexible whereas the RNN is fixed and modifications are not feasible.

Low cost sensors namely Kinect and LMC are also used along with NN techniques. Mohandes et al. (2014) used MLPNN to extract twelve features and Bayes classifier to recognize 28 samples. They produced accuracy 99.1% with the help of LMC sensor. The 3D Convolutional Neural Network was introduced by Molchanov et al. (2015) to recognize the hand gestures using Kinect and produced only 77.5% recognition accuracy for 19 gestures. Unanue et al. (2017) used RNN to initialize the features and to pre-train the embeddings of features. However in the field of SLR, HMMs has given successful results compared with other researches in the perspective of recognizing and classifying temporal features.

2.4.2. *Hidden Markov Models*

Hidden Markov Models are the stochastic techniques to analyze the spatiotemporal data with varying time signals i.e. dynamic gestures (Ouhyoung & Liang 1996) of SLR. Vision-based recognition was introduced by Grobel & Assan (1997) for isolated signs and prove their system provides strong classification results using HMM under the constraints designed for the implementation. Coupled HMMs (CHMM) was introduced by Brand et al. (1997) and Factorial HMMs (FHMM) was introduced by Ghahramani & Jordan (1996) to improve the performance of standard HMMs and compare the performance with linked HMMs (Vogler & Metaxas 1997). They proved that their system was least sensitive while there was less sufficient training data and stochastic independent assumptions.

The Parametric HMM (PHMM) was introduced by Wilson & Bobick (1999) to improve the performance of parameter-based system when compared to regular HMM. Vogler & Metaxas (1999) introduced Parallel HMMs (PaHMM) and the later used Ong & Ranganath (2004) and Von Agris et al. (2008) to solve the inherent analogous nature of the linguistic components. They proved in their work that their proposed approach outperformed CHMM, FHMM and Standard HMMs. This concept was used to train 400 sentences and test 99 sentences (Vogler et al. 2007). They produced accuracy 94.23% in recognizing isolated signs and 84.85% accuracy in recognizing continuous signs.

Input/output HMMs (IOHMMs) was introduced by Bengio & Frasconi (1996) to observe multiple sequences and to handle inhomogeneous structures. Marcel at el. (2000) used IOHMMs to classify the hand trajectories without any information to hand shape. Just et al. (2004) used IOHMMs to recognize the 16 motion based gestures without shape variation and produced 74% accuracy in recognizing the 3D hand gestures. Keskin & Akarun (2009) extended the idea of IOHMM with threshold based model and they have produced an accuracy of over 90 percent for vary small dataset consist of 10 to 20 gestures even after using the hardware and interface devices. Liu & Lovell (2003) introduced and experimented different structure model of HMM namely Left-Right HMM. But the experimental results proved that the system had no effect on the accuracy.

Elmezian et al. (2008) & Elmezian et al. (2009) combined GMM with HMM to recognize the isolated hand gestures and to classify the meaningful information. Even though, HMM model used GMM for data distribution, when training data are too low, the system performance will degrade immediately. Appenrodt et al. (2010) also used HMM to recognize the hand gestures with the help of stereo-cameras. However, all these three systems could not be directly applied to SLR systems.

There are some recent approaches which combine HMM with other techniques to improve the performance. Zaki & Shaheen (2011) combined HMM with PCA as a measure of calculating hand configuration and orientation of sign features. Barros et al. (2013) used HMM with RNN to extract hand contour using Speeded Up Robust Feature (SURF). However, this approach works with the fixed gestures and not robust for the newly introduced gestures. Fast HMM was introduced by Yang et al. (2016) and combined with level building algorithm to improve the recognition performance. However, their system performance will improve only with employing grammar and sign length constraints. Belgacem et al. (2017) combined conditional random fields with HMM to satisfy the needs of low training data. But this model still involves complex detection due to the presence of large number of states.

2.4.3. Other Classification Approaches

Some of the notable classification approaches of SLR include K-Nearest Neighbour, Support Vector Machine (SVM), Relevance Vector Machine (RVM), K-Means Clustering, Dynamic Time Warping and Self Organizing Map (SOM). Wang & Popovic (2009) proposed a real-time hand tracking application using coloured gloves. They used KNN approach to recognize the colour pattern of the gloves. However, their system required only continuous hand streams. Also, KNN is compared with Support Vector Machine (Kurdyumov et al. 2011, Rekha et al. 2011, Tharwat et al. 2015, Baranwal & Nandi 2017) and all these systems have proved that the SVM based approaches outperforms the KNN approaches. However, the SVM based approaches will classify only the static gestures and it requires more number of features to train the systems.

Wong & Cipla (2005) have proved that the RVM machines with the probabilistic nature of Bayesian classifier have produced more accurate results in complex motion analysis whereas the SVM based approaches the true or false while recognizing the motions. But their system requires more training data and recognizes only 10 gestures. To overcome the need of more training data and to enable the system to recognize larger number of vocabularies, some researchers have used K-means Clustering (Coogan & Sutherland 2006, Schmitt & McCoy 2011, Dardas & Georganas 2011) to cluster the features and then used these features as input to SVM classifier. To reduce the bag of features, Fuzzy k-means clustering (Zhang et al. 2011) was used with the fusion of accelerometer and 5-channel Electromyography. Using this setup, 72 gestures of Chinese Sign Language (CSL) have been recognized with the accuracy 93.1%. Fuzzy k-means clustering was adapted by Anderson et al. (2017) and combined orientation classifier to classify the sign gestures. However, this technique is also more reliable for spatial features.

To compute the effective distance between the temporal sequences, Dynamic Time Warping (Darrell & Pentland 1993) was introduced to recognize 4 sign gestures from continuous video sequences and achieve 96% accuracy in recognition. After the effective recognition, some more hybrid approaches were introduced. Statistical DTW (SDTW) was combined by Lichtenauer et al. (2008) with two other classifiers that include Combined Discriminative Feature Detectors (CDFD) and Quadratic Classification on DF Fisher Mapping. This method showed improved accuracy than the simple DTW. However, all the considered features were not important in classification. In gesture recognition (Rekha et al. 2011), SDTW techniques warp an observed motion of pre-stored joint gestures. To select the important features, Celebi et al. (2013) followed Weighted DTW (WDTW) proposed by (Rayes et al. 2011) along with the Kinect sensor to extract the joints based on the weighted signals of two sequences. But they recognized only 20 gestures and also their system faced difficulty in handling the feature vectors of varied length based on the obtained gesture class.

Parametric Derivative Dynamic Time Warping (DDTW) was introduced by Górecki & Łuczak (2015) to obtain the hand shape features. However, their system consumed more time in the learning phase. Yang et al. (2016) introduced Fast HMM and combined it with level building based DTW algorithm to improve the recognition performance. However, their system performance improved only with employing grammar and sign length constraints. Self-Organizing Maps (SOM) was employed by Caridakis et al. (2012) and combined HMM (Fang et al. 2004, Gao et al. 2004) to solve the problem spatiotemporal feature extraction. However, their system had the limitation of working only for isolated signs and it was not possible in the case of continuous sentences to segment the trajectory boundaries. Recurrent SOM was introduced by Sun et al. (2016) to extract the spatial features and combined with DTW to collect the temporal sequences. However, this approach is developed to recognize the human activity nor for SLR system.

The proposed system introduces a novel Bayesian Parallel Hidden Markov Model (BPHMM) to combine manual and non-manual features classified using Parallel HMM and it also handles the problem of movement ambiguities using dynamic pruning of clustering with DTW. This proposed BPaHMM combines the visual and linguistic transcriptions of sign lexicon along with extracted manual and non-manual features to form a subunit gesture base. The feature vectors are extracted based on both spatial and temporal feature groups to form the subunit gesture base. In this work, shape-based features and region-based features are considered as subunit-manual spatial feature vectors. At the same time, motion trajectories are estimated to form the subunit-manual temporal feature vectors. The facial parameters namely shape and texture information are extracted to structure the subunit-non-manual feature vectors. Extraction of manual and non-manual features using subunit modelling helps to resolve the movement ambiguities and occlusions which are considered as the most important issues in real world sign language recognition.

2.5. Modelling and Recognition of Sign Language

In general, Sign language recognition can be categorized as isolated sign recognition and continuous sentence recognition. Similarly, the SLR system can be modelled as whole sign level modelling and subunit level sign modelling. In turn, subunit level sign modelling can be achieved using either of the two approaches: linguistic-oriented approach and visual-descriptive approach. Also, while recognizing the sign gestures two factors need to be considered which includes signer dependence/independence and large vocabulary of sign gestures.

2.5.1. Isolated Sign Recognition

Isolated signs are performed as a letter or a word at a time. The recognition approach involves different sign languages. Pugeault & Bowden (2011) have presented a framework for isolated sign recognition of 26 ASL alphabets and produced an accuracy of 75%. The authors addressed the ambiguity but the system needs clear pauses. To overcome this issue, Dominio et al. (2014) implemented the gesture recognition based on curvature of hand shapes and recognize 12 ASL signs with an accuracy of 97.60%.

Based on Kinect sensor, there are a few systems (Keskin et al. 2012, Pedersoli et al. 2014, Kirac et al. 2014) developed to recognize 24 letters of the ASL alphabet. But the accuracy of all the systems still needs to be improved. There are some recent SLR approaches combining with LMC to recognize isolated words (Marin et al. 2014, Marin et al. 2016). In the former approach, they use fingertip information and correlates with SVM to get the accuracy of 91.28% for 10 ASL digits whereas in the latter approach, they use extracts of 3D information and correlates with SVM. This system shows the better accuracy of 96.50% for 10 ASL digits.

A framework for isolated sign recognition of German Sign Language (GSL) was presented by Lang et al. (2012) using depth-camera and produced an accuracy of 97% for 25 signs. Potter et al. (2013) used LMC to recognize 26 Australian Sign Language (AUSLAN) using 3D finger points and ANN. Zhang et al. (2011) extracted velocity and statistical features using sensor glove with HMM and produced 92.50% accuracy for 72 Chinese words. However, these systems cannot recognize complex inputs. Almeida et al. (2014) recognized Brazilian Sign Language (BSL) of 34 signs and produced an accuracy of 80% with Kinect Sensor.

A SLR system for Indian Sign Language (ISL) was proposed by Nandy et al. (2010) and recognized 22 ISL signs with 92.29% accuracy. Rekha et al. (2011) produced 91.30% of accuracy for 26 ISL gestures using 2D computer vision techniques. However, their proposed approach suffered from varying illuminations. Mehrotra et al. (2015) recognized 37 ISL signs and attained an accuracy of 86.16% based on 3D skeleton point's features from Kinect sensor using SVM. Kumar et al. (2017) recognized 50 ISL signs using Kinect and LMC sensors and attained the accuracy of 40.23% for all sign gestures. However, all the developed systems recognize only the isolated words and include only manual features. It is mandatory for the SLR system to include both manual and non-manual parameters to produce an accurate result.

More recently, a number of researches evolved in Arabic Sign Language (ArSL) recognition. To solve the problem of hand occlusion (Al-Roussan et al. 2009) in isolated signs, Al-Roussan et al. (2010) introduced two-stage scheme of HMM classifier. However, the occluded objects removal based on previous assumption of tracked objects is not possible in the real-time. Ahmed & Aly (2014) used the combination of PCA and local binary patterns to extract the features of 23 isolated ArSL signs. However, their system produced an accuracy of 99.97% in signer dependent mode and it failed to recognize the constant gray-scale patterns in the signing area due to the usage of threshold operator. Ibrahim et al. (2017) recognized 30 isolated Arabic signs and obtained an accuracy of 97%. However, to attain better results and performance and to implement in real-time continuous sign sentences all the methods need to be improved. Table 2.1 lists some of the existing approaches of isolated and continuous SLR system along with feature extraction and classification techniques.

Table 2.1: Summary of Sign Language Recognition Approaches

References	Sign Vocabulary/ Modelling	Sign Modelling Level	Feature Extraction	Classification	Accuracy (%)
Almeida et.al (2014)	BSL/ Isolated	Phoneme	RGB-D Sensors – Manual	SVM	80%
Tubaiz et.al (2015)	ArSL/ Continuous	Sign	DG5-VHand data gloves- Manual	Modified KNN	98.9% (80 word lexicon)
Han et.al (2009)	British SL/ Isolated	Subunit	Computer Vision- Manual (Motion)	DTW	99% (20 signs)
Yin et.al (2009)	ASL/ Isolated	Phoneme	Accelerometer - Data-Driven Fenemes	DIST-SBHMM	60% (single hand)
Shanableh et.al (2007)	ArSL/ Isolated	Sign	Computer Vision- Manual	Bayesian+ KNN	93% (23 signs)
Gao et.al (2004)	CSL/ Isolated	Sign	Computer Vision- Manual	SOFM+SRN +HMM	82.9% (5113 signs)
Caridakis et.al (2014)	ASL/ Isolated	Sign	Computer Vision- NonManual	RNN+HMM	79%
Oz & Leu (2011)	ASL/ Isolated	Sign	Cyber Glove + Flock of Birds- 3D Motion – Manual	ANN	93%
Proposed	**ASL + GSL / Isolated + Continuous**	**Subunit**	**Computer Vision- Manual + Non-Manual Features**	**BPaHMM**	**91% (5356 sentences) and 98.64% (3300 signs)**

2.5.2. Continuous Sign Recognition

Continuous Sign Recognition involves recognizing one or more complete sentences or finger spelled signs as continuous data. In continuous sign recognition, not only the problem of occlusion occurs but also the problem of identifying the sign gestures from the transition movements, i.e. epentheses movements. The automatic recognition of epentheses movements is required to extend the recognition from isolated signs to continuous signs. However, there are no clear pauses between the signs in continuous SLR the segmentation of epentheses movements are intractable. Several typical research works are presented in eliminating epentheses movements by explicit modelling, implicit modelling or by simply ignoring the epentheses movements.

2.5.2.1. *Explicit Modelling of Epentheses Movements*

To remove transition movements, explicit modelling with HMM was carried out (Vogler & Metaxas 2004, Kelly et al. 2009, Han et al. 2013) but the limitation arises in detecting sign boundaries. Also, they had many constraints in the training data for limited data corpus. Context-dependent model (Yuan et al. 2002, Gao et al. 2004) to handle epentheses movements were discussed and used the training data to pre-cluster these transition movements. Bauer & Kraiss (2002) used k-means clustering along with HMM to recognize and cluster epentheses movements but the direct HMM failed in generalizing transitions when vocabulary grows large. Another segmentation model for removing epentheses movements was introduced by Ong & Ranganath (2005) which lies in creating general rules for boundary calculation but it is not applicable for all types of gestures.

Transition Movement Model (TMM) was developed by Fang et al. (2007) to handle large vocabulary CSL of 5113 Chinese signs and produced an accuracy of 91.9%. However, their approach requires data gloves for data acquisition and pre-processing. Also, it requires more computation time to model the epentheses movements before processing the sign gestures. Another novel segment and merge- based probabilistic approach was introduced (Kong & Ranganath 2014) based on sign sub-segments and produced 81.6% accuracy in spotting the sign gestures but the movement epentheses need to be labelled manually. Koller et al. (2015) developed CSLR for recognizing the GSL of two data corpus and reported an error rate up to 50% in recognizing the sign gestures.

2.5.2.2. *Implicit Modelling of Epentheses Movements*

Certain other approaches were also developed in earlier experiments to segment epentheses movements without any explicit modelling. Starner et al. (1998) trained HMM with each word or phoneme. In both the works, the authors trained the full sentence instead of individual signs. This leads to the loss of valid sign because all the epentheses movements cannot be trained and fluency of individual signer will also vary for large vocabulary signs. Yang et al. (2010) developed an enhanced level building algorithm to handle epentheses movements and hand segmentation ambiguities. They produced recognition accuracy around 90% for 10 sentences but their system required more groundwork for manual labeling of signs and epentheses movements.

The concept of movement prime using three-dimensional data in HMM was introduced (Nam & Wohn 1996, Nam & Wohn 1999) to recognize continuous signs and the similar concepts of phoneme approaches was later used by Neidle et al. (2014) to remove epentheses movements. More recently, Li et al. (2016) presented a scalable approach by simply ignoring transition movements and their system gives an accuracy of around 87%. But their proposed approach dealt only with the small vocabulary and it requires more time for finding the matching pattern. Yang et al. (2016) developed an extended approach (Yang et al. 2010) to overcome the problem of distance computation at each level in level-building algorithm using Fast HMM. However, their approach used Kinect sensor for data acquisition. Also, it does not incorporate the hand shape feature which is the most essential feature in classifying the sign gestures and it requires more running time due to level building approach.

2.5.2.3. Multimodal Recognition

There are some recent approaches which recognized both the continuous and the isolated signs; and also the SLR systems are developed to recognize multi-lingual signs. Product HMM was used by Theodorakis et al. (2009) for the recognition of Greek signs using asynchronous combination of features and proved that their system outperformed the synchronous modality combination. A multimodal fusion technique was introduced by Aaran et al. (2009) to extract the manual and non-manual features. However, their system was considered only the second decision based on the confidence level of first information. So many misclassifications occurred in identifying the sign gestures from continuous data stream. Yang & Lee (2013) integrated manual and non-manual features using Hierarchical-Conditional Random Field (HCRF). Their approach was tested against 98 continuous ASL sentences and produced an accuracy of 84.1%. However, their approach cannot be used because of ambiguity occurrences.

Forster et al. (2013) used PaHMMs (Deng et al. 2002, Wang et al. 2006) to recognize the sign gestures of ASL and CSL modalities and produced over 90% accuracy. However their modalities are not considered for asynchronous data of continuous sentences. Ong et al. (2014) recognized British SL, German SL and ASL using feature selection from the decision trees and produced 71% accuracy in recognition. Their approach seemed producing promising results but on continuous data it faced difficulties in producing synchronous results. Kinect sensor and LMC was used by Kumar et al. (2018) for extracting the multimodal features and produced an accuracy of 94.27%

for ISL sign words. However, their approach included more features and did not select any robust features to reduce the time complexity.

2.5.3. *Signer Adaptation*

Although the latest research in SLR focused on large corpus signer dependent approaches, there are some approaches which focused on experimenting cross-signer validation. The foremost problem in recognition is recitation of the system that is adapting the independent or native signer when the systems have not been trained on them. The reason behind this problem is data collection. Many existing approaches require a large number of data for training the SLR system, if the approaches use data gloves, the correctness and validity of the system cannot be determined directly. Similarly, if the approaches use computer vision techniques, many professionals are required for data collection and all of them are required to do large-vocabulary sentences. And also, the number of signers in the training set is small, unseen signer recognition accuracy will be severely tainted.

The SLR approach to show the importance of signer independence was proposed by Zieren & Kraiss (2005). Their approach faced difficulties in selecting the features and identifying unseen signers. Also, they have showed that their system produced better results for trained signers and suddenly the recognition performance dropped from 99.3% to 44.1% for 221 signs of unseen signers in real-time environments. Maximum Posterior (MAP) Estimation and Maximum Linear Likelihood Regression (MLLR) was combined by Von Agris et al. (2008) for signer adaptation and showed the signer independent recognition accuracy of 65.3% for 780 sentences.

To solve the problem of lack of training samples in SLR, Jiang et al. (2009) introduced a synthetic data driving method and used mean shift algorithm to solve the problem of signer adaptation. Their approach yielded 82.86% accuracy for 5113 isolated Chinese words. To recognize the letters of the alphabet, Pattanaworapan & Chamnongthai (2012) classified the fingers based on fully extended and curled fingers using the threshold value on finger state detection. Due to various hand sizes, their approach could not handle unseen signer validation and produced an accuracy of around 61%. Mohandes et al. (2012) developed Gaussian skin colour segmentation based signer-independent SLR system for three signers consists of 300 words and they reported that their system produced 95% accuracy without any deviation from signer dependent mode. However, their recognition performance increases only when the number of training samples is getting increased i.e. for one word it requires 30 training samples.

More recently, an SLR system to support signer adaptation based on novel Active Appearance Model (AAM) was developed by Koller et al. (2015). They evaluated the proposed approach in two datasets: 1) SIGNUM-laboratory restricted dataset and 2) RWTH-PHOENIX-Weather-unconstrained real-life dataset. Even though their approach showed 16.4% error rate in laboratory set up, it showed 53% error rate in unrestricted environment which would highly affect the recognition performance of SLR. Pattanaworapan et al. (2016) used DWT and 1D signal for modelling the SLR system. Their approach showed an accuracy of over 88% in non-fist based gestures and in fist based gestures, it showed an accuracy of over 58%. Kim et al. (2017) presented lexicon free SLR using Segmental Conditional Random Field (SCRF) and Deep Neural Network (DNN). However, their approach produced 92% accuracy in the case of signer dependent mode and showed reduced accuracy of 83% for multi-signer recognition. Table 2.2 lists the comparative summary of modelling epentheses movement and signer adaptation.

Table 2.2: Comparative Summary on Modelling Epentheses Movement and Signer Adaptation

References	Implicit/ Explicit/ Ignored	Isolated / Continuous	Sign Level/ Subunit Level	Modelling	Cross-Signer Validation
Vogler & Metaxas (2001)	Explicit	Isolated	Phoneme	HMM	No
Yuan et. al (2002)	Explicit	Continuous	Sub-word	HMM	No
Fang et. al (2007)	Explicit	Isolated	Sign	K-means	No
Yang et. al (2009)	Explicit	Continuous	Sign	CRF + Epentheses THMM	No
Kelly et. al (2011)	Explicit	Isolated	Sign	GTHMM	No
Kong & Ranganath (2014)	Segment + Merge	Continuous	Sub-segments	SVM + Semi-Markov CRF	No
Yang et. al (2010)	Manual labelling	Continuous	Sign	Enhanced Level Building	Yes
Pitsikalis et. al (2011)	Phonetic Based	Isolated	Phoneme	HamNoSys	No
Li et.al (2016)	Ignored	Isolated + Continuous	Sign	HMM	Yes
Proposed	**Pre-Cluster**	**Isolated + Continuous**	**Subunit**	**SMP-HMM, MEC+DTW**	**Yes**

*SMP-HMM (Subunit Multi-stream Parallel-HMM)

2.5.4. Subunit Sign Modelling

To achieve better performance in automatic sign language recognition, many efforts were made to recognize subunits in the past decade. Subunits are formed by breaking the whole signs into smaller sub-units. Unlike speech recognition, for over a past decade there has been no standard forms available for modelling and constructing the subunits. Based on the previous researches, Subunit sign modelling can be done in two ways: Linguistic-oriented approach and visual-oriented approach.

2.5.4.1. Linguistic-Oriented Approach

The linguistic-oriented approach is initially derived by Stokoe (1991) based on the linguistic syllable. The word chreme was coined by Stokoe (2005) to construct sign lexicon, however, without manual alterations, the syllables cannot be used as a gesture base for Sign Language Recognition. Since the chremes are performed in parallel apart from sign actions, the movements are also labeled as subunits. Stokoe's chremes was followed by Kadir et al. (2004) to classify the signs and they have introduced a two-stage classification model for recognizing sign language. Liddell & Johnson (1989) introduced the movement-hold model; the signs are separated in linear order into fragments. Similar to Stokoe (2005) notation, no such sign lexicon is available. Moreover, these sequential definitions create additional problems in video processing. Cooper & Bowden (2010) developed linguistic oriented recognition system, but the subunits were acquired manually. The authors have combined these subunit classifiers and adopted Markov models to recognize the signs.

The movement-hold model was followed by Vogler & Metaxas (2001) which was originally proposed by Liddell & Johnson (1989) and used Hidden Markov Model for the phoneme level sign recognition. Yeasin & Chaudri (2000) also followed the movement-hold model and used finite state machines to model the state durations. The major drawback of this system is it needs clear breaks between two consecutive signs, but it is not possible with frequent signers. Theodorakis et.al (2010) proposed data driven clustering approach to drive subunits regardless of solving subunit-based recognition.

Some of the recent approaches have focussed on breaking up signs into subunits based on linguistics to allow the scalability on large vocabulary datasets. Earlier, this attempt was started by Waldron & Kim (1995) to recognize isolated ASL signs. Hanke (2004) introduced HamNoSys notation for linguistic representation of signs. Inspired by this concept, Pitsikalis et al. (2011) used HamNoSys to extract subunit definition from the annotated linguistic dataset for recognizing isolated Greek SL. Sutton (2000) introduced another sign notation named

SignWriting and it was used by Koller et al. (2013) to recognize the GSL and to align the linguistically derived subunits as meaningful signs.

2.5.4.2. *Visual-Oriented Approach*

Although many researches focussed on using linguistic descriptions of signs and constructing the standard dictionary for writing the signs, none of the system produced effective results and also, the practical implementation of such linguistic-oriented approach is highly infeasible. To overcome the infeasibility in linguistic-oriented approach, another method of visual-oriented approach was adapted. Fang et al. (2004) extracted subunits for sign language recognition using data glove approach. This method relies on HMM model in such a way that one HMM for one subunit. Dynamic Bayesian network was employed by Ong & Ranganath (2005) to model the systematic variations for different signs as parallel cues with independent features, and later they combined these cues as subunits.

Derpanis et al. (2008) derived mapping between phonemic and kinematic visual motions to recognize isolated movement phonemes. Bauer and Kraiss (2001) proposed a clustering algorithm for self-organizing subunits using spatial features as individual frames (SU-F). This approach ignores the temporal feature which is one of the essential features to recognize sign gestures. Han et al. (2009) derived subunits from hand action in time and space based on hand motion boundary and correlated the obtained subunits with linguistic syllables. But their approach required more training samples irrespective of the gesture size. To overcome this, Han et al. (2013) proposed boosted subunit framework for recognizing isolated signs. Nevertheless, this framework left the problem unsolved for a large set of vocabulary.

Theodorakis et al. (2014) introduced the concept of dynamic and static subunits (2-S-U) to derive the subunits and acquired an accuracy of around 95% in signer dependent recognition and 63% in signer independent recognition. However, their approach required more computation time due to late integration of hand shape subunits. Koller et al. (2016) introduced subunit sign modelling based on Subunit and imagent-hand motion (SU-IMH). However, pre-training for motion of hands is required for their approach due to lack of information model in Convolutional Neural Networks (CNN). Cooper et al. (2017) also used linguistically extracted subunits without any separation on spatial and temporal features (SU-noST) and compared the results of 3D tracking information using boosted sequential trees for recognizing British SL.

The proposed automatic sign language classification and recognition system contributes to the following four aspects: (1) First; the proposed work uses data-driven approach for sequential and parallel break down of signs into subunits without any prior knowledge about gestures. (2) The proposed system introduces Bayesian Parallel Hidden Markov Model to combine manual and non-manual subunit features, and it also handles the problem of movement ambiguities. (3) The proposed work adopts intra-gloss sign lexicon to construct gesture base where similar features of different signs are shared and stored. (4) Finally, regardless of the signer dependence, the proposed work handles various signers under different illuminations in real world sign language recognition. Table 2.3 summarizes the differences between some of the existing subunit based sign recognition and proposed approach.

Table 2.3: Comparison of Different Subunit Sign Modelling

References	Subunit Modelling	Subunit Segmentation	Modelling	Cross-Signer Validation
Vogler & Metaxas (2001)	Implicit	NA	Context- Dependent HMM+Epentheses	No
Kadir et al. (2004)		Rule-Based	Sequential Pattern Boosting	Yes
Ong & Ranganath (2005)		NA	MLP/HMM	No
Theodorakis et al. (2010)		DIST-SBHMMS	HMM	No
Han et al. (2013)		Motion Trajectories	AdaBoost + weak classifiers	No
Bauer & Kraiss (2001)	Explicit	K-Means	HMM	No
Fang et al. (2004)		Left to Right-HMM	Modified K-Means, DTW, HMM	No
Cooper & Bowden (2007)		NA	Parallel HMM + Epentheses	No
Kong & Ranganath (2014)		Rule-Based	HMM	No
Theodorakis et al. (2014)		2 state Ergodic HMM	Parallel HMM	Yes
Proposed	**NA**	**BPaHMM**	**Multistream Parallel HMM**	**Yes**

2.6. Sign Corpus

Sign Corpus involves the collection of sign data to form the gesture base to be used in SL recognition. Recent researches involved SLR recognizing the large vocabulary data corpus. There are several benchmark datasets available for SLR in different sign languages. For British Sign Language, there are several data corpus: RWTH-Boston-10, RWTH-Boston-50 (Zahedi et al. 2005), RWTH-Boston-104 (Dreuw et al. 2007, Dreuw et al. 2008) and RWTH-Boston-400. It consists of 10, 50, 104 and 400 British signs respectively. For GSL, DGS Kinect-40 (Cooper et al. 2012, Ong et al. 2012), RWTH-German Finger Spelling (Dreuw et al. 2006), SIGNUM (Koller et al. 2015) and RWTH-PHOENIX-Weather (Forster et al. 2012, Forster et al. 2014, Koller et al. 2013, Koller et al. 2015) datasets are available. They consist of 40 signs, 35 signs, 455 signs (around 19K Sentences signed by 9 native signers) and 1225 signs (5356 continuous sentences signed by 9 native signers, publicly available annotated with start and end frame of face and hand) respectively. For Greek Sign Language, GSL 20 dataset (Cooper et al. 2012, Ong et al. 2012, Ong et al. 2014) is available and it consists of 20 isolated words signed by six native signers.

American Sign Language Lexicon Video Dataset (ASLLVD) is the most commonly used ASL dataset (Thangali et al. 2011, Dilsizian et al. 2014) which includes more than 33K isolated signs signed by six native signers. It is a publicly available dataset which is annotated with start frames and end frames of hands. For Polish Sign Language (PSL), three different datasets are available namely PSL Kinect 30 (Oszust & Wysocki 2013, Oszust & Wysocki 2014, Kapuscinski et al. 2015), PSL ToF 84 (Oszust & Wysocki 2013, Kapuscinski et al. 2015) and PSL 101 (Oszust & Wysocki 2012) whereas these data sets consists of 30 signs, 84 signs and 101 signs and all these isolated words are done by one native signer. For Indian Sign Language, IITA-ROBITA ISL (Nandy et al. 2010, Rekha et al. 2011, Kumar et al. 2017) there is one developed by Indian Institute of Technology Allahabad, with 23 sign gestures signed by one native signer. Among these data, the unrestricted datasets namely ASLLVD and RWTH-PHOENIX-Weather datasets are chosen in the proposed subunit sign modelling approach to prove the efficiency of recognizing large corpus data under unconstrained environments.

2.7. Summary

Based on state-of-art, the book Subunit Sign Modelling for Continuous Sign Language concentrates on solving three major issues namely extraction and selection of robust subunit features, handling epentheses movements and implementing the framework for subunit sign modelling. The first contribution at the feature level, considers the problem that makes hand segmentation and grouping hard which includes using short sleeves, signing in complex background and interaction without external interface devices. The second contribution at the sentence level considers the problem of handling epentheses movements that are pruning epentheses movements and classifying sign gestures. The final contribution of the book is the introducing of a novel subunit sign modelling and signer adaptation framework for automatic sign language recognition system to recognize large vocabulary which involves subunit extraction, subunit sign lexicon construction, subunit sharing and sign classification.

CHAPTER III

3. Proposed Subunit Sign Modelling Architecture

3.1. Introduction

This chapter of the dissertation depicts the proposed subunit sign modelling framework architecture for continuous sign language recognition. The working nature of each components involved in the proposed research work are explained in this chapter. This chapter also describes the system implementation based on the training and exploitation phase and experimental set up of the proposed framework.

The proposed framework consists of five major components namely Pre-Processing, Subunit (SU) Extraction, Spatial/Temporal(S/T) SU Modelling, SU Sign Lexicon Construction and SU training and Recognition. The following sections elaborate the individual elements of the major components of the proposed framework. Figure 3.1 illustrates the proposed subunit sign modelling framework for continuous sign language recognition.

3.2. Pre-Processing

Pre-Processing is the most essential part in recognizing the sign languages. It is responsible for processing the front signing videos consisting of isolated signs and continuous sentences and producing the extracted features for further processing of subunits. These features are going to serve as the input for subunit extraction.

3.2.1. Skin Pixel Identification

Skin pixel identification (hand and face localization) and tracking are performed by identifying skin pixels in the area of interest. A hand tracking algorithm is proposed which is simple, efficient and also easy to understand so that it can be applied to real time applications. This algorithm is based on the colour detection and motion of the hand.

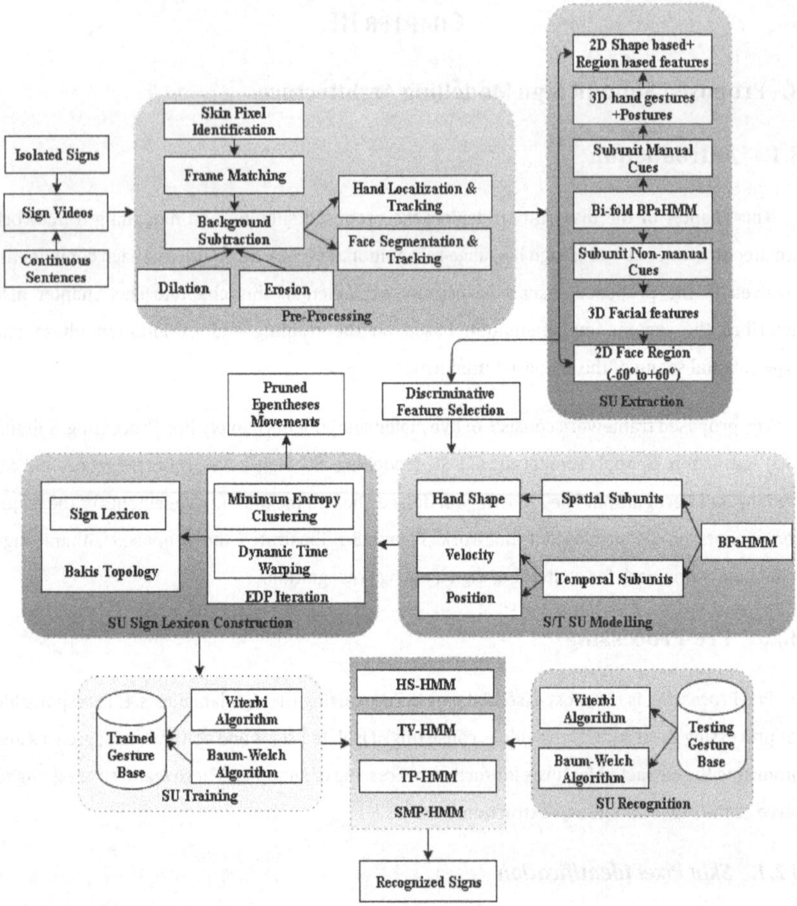

Figure 3.1: Subunit Sign Modelling Framework for Continuous Sign Language Recognition

3.2.2. Frame Matching

Frame matching step is used to analyse the trajectories of the hands from one frame to another frame. The extracted frames are converted into gray scale images, then a frame matching algorithm is used to analyse the movement of the hand direction. In this stage, the static background is subtracted in the dynamic video sequence.

3.2.3. Background Subtraction

Background subtraction is used to eliminate the noise in the extracted frames. It involved in two subsequent processes namely erosion and dilation.

- Erosion: Erosion process is used to reduce the noise in the frames of the unaided video sequence.
- Dilation: Once the erosion is done, Dilation is used to manipulate the geographical area of the frames.

3.2.4. Hand and Face Segmentation and Tracking

Hand and face localization and tracking are performed by identifying skin pixels in the area of interest. After localization and tracking, the manual and non-manual features are extracted to represent the position and trajectories of hand with respect to the head position to locate the signs in the given video sequences.

The centroid coordinate of the frames is extracted with reference to head position to construct the feature groups of temporal subunits whereas the shape features are estimated based on Fourier transform to construct the spatial subunits. Finally, both the features are given as input to the Hidden Markov Model to classify the sign gestures.

3.3. SU Extraction

Subunit extraction involves the sequential and parallel breakdown of sign gestures without any prior knowledge on syllables and number of subunits. The manual and non-manual features are extracted using Parallel Hidden Markov Model. These feature vectors are sequentially segmented and simultaneously given as the input signals to Parallel HMM to classify the subunits. Based on the output state of PaHMM, Bi-fold Bayesian network is constructed by merging the subunits from manual and non-manual feature groups to form subunit gesture base.

3.3.1. Bayesian Parallel Hidden Markov Model

A novel Bayesian Parallel Hidden Markov Model is introduced for subunit extraction. This proposed BPaHMM combines the visual and linguistic transcriptions of sign lexicon along with extracted manual and non-manual features to form a subunit gesture base.

3.3.1.1. Manual Features

Manual feature groups are formed from the feature vectors of hand gestures. Manual feature groups are constructed by the breakdown of hand signals and sign sequence into subunits without any prior information about knowledge source like the movement-hold model. In fact, a subunit is represented by a feature group with different feature vectors.

Subunit spatial features are derived from shape based and region based information. In this work, the shape-based features namely Fourier descriptors and curvature representors are considered whereas for the region-based features, the moments and moment-based invariants are considered. They all together form the subunit spatial feature vectors. Similarly, subunit temporal features estimated from the hand trajectory vectors namely hand position, hand orientation and hand velocity are also considered.

3.3.1.2. Non-Manual Features

Non-manual feature groups are generally constructed from the feature vectors of upper body posture. In sign language recognition, certain signs are similar according to its manual gesture and such signs can be identified only with the help of non-manual parameters. The PaHMM model for non-manual feature vector is constructed in such a way that each feature vector represents one subunit. The essential feature vectors to construct the non-manual features are face shape and head pose estimation.

3.3.2. Discriminative Feature Selection

The efficacy of multiple features and their combinations is evaluated to find the most prompting feature combination and to improve the efficiency of the recognition rate. First, the estimation is done on the individual features and then several combinations of the selected features are tested and the results are evaluated. Based on the discriminative feature selection from the extracted robust features, three features namely hand shape, velocity and position are identified as important features to reduce the feature space and computation time.

3.4. S/T SU Modelling

The major concern in SU sign modelling is segmenting signs into sub-sign segments and classifying such segments as S/T SUs. A Bayesian Network is employed to handle the classification of spatial and temporal subunits. This classification is purely based on hand movements and postures. After that, a HMM model is adapted to recombine these subunits where the first state corresponds to spatial subunits and the second state corresponds to temporal subunits.

3.4.1. Spatial Subunits

The spatial SUs are considered as static postures which do not involve in any transitions. The spatial subunits are constructed from hand shape which is selected as one of the discriminative features based on the feature selection strategy.

3.4.2. Temporal Subunits

The temporal subunits are the dynamic gestures and those involved in transitions. The temporal subunits are constructed from position and velocity cues of hands during transitions. These features are also selected from the discriminative feature selection strategy.

3.4.3. Construction of S/T SUs

S/T SUs are clustered after the segmentation and modelled with Multi-stream Parallel HMM. Spatial Subunits are constructed based on extracted hand shape using the Fourier descriptors. Once all the SUs are obtained, all the frames are considered to cluster with MEC where each clusters corresponding to different SUs.

Temporal subunits are constructed by considering the transition movements. Based on the velocity of transition, the subunit is considered as hand velocity or hand position. By calculating the average frequency of frames i.e. 30 key frames per second, the frame with high transition movement is treated as velocity cue where as the frames with less transition movements are treated as position SUs. Before forming the sign lexicon, the direction or the scale of the feature vectors with respect to the initial position are normalized to obtain effective normalized segments to incorporate model invariance.

3.5. SU Sign Lexicon Construction

Sign Lexicon is constructed without any prior knowledge on phonetic transcriptions, annotations or manual labelling. Data-Driven approach is followed to construct the sign lexicon by combining hand shape, position and velocity features. These are obtained from S/T SU construction and then the constructed lexicon is used for SU training and recognition. After segmenting and clustering S/T SUs, it is united together to get the lexicon. By this way, the sign lexicon consists of an entry in the gesture base for each SU. Every SU in the gesture base consists of Spatial (S) or Temporal (T) SU label along with the assigned cluster id.

3.5.1. EDP Iteration

This research work mainly concentrates on handling epentheses movements between adjacent signs; clustering only the spatial features will result in poor classification of sign gestures. To make effective classification and segmentation of sign gestures, temporal features are also considered while clustering. These temporal series of signs are calculated using the dynamic time warping technique as a distance measure between the two adjacent signs. This clustering process is done iteratively to remove all the epentheses movement. This component is named as the Enhanced Dynamic Programming (EDP) iteration since it adapts the features of dynamic programming and spatiotemporal clustering.

3.5.2. *Gesture Base*

Based on the construction of S/T SUs and sign lexicon generation, the trained gesture base is formed. The gesture base consists of sign lexica based on spatial and temporal cue segmentation along with the cluster id. As a result, similar hand shapes of different signs are clustered accordingly. This allows the gesture base to be shared by two or more similar SUs.

3.6. SU Training and Recognition

According to the constructed sign lexicon, each sign is composed of a sequence of S/T SUs. For training and recognition of SU, a Subunit Multi-stream Hidden Markov Model (SMP-HMM) is used. In recognition, the most probable S/T segment needs to be found from the given set of features and from the SU models that best match the S/T segment.

3.6.1. *SMP-HMM*

In the SMP-HMM model, the S/T segments by using TV cues, TP cues and S cues for the dominant hand. Similarly, it integrates all the cues for the non-dominant hands. Because HMM alone cannot manage all these cues, Multi-stream HMM are used to train these set of features but the features are segmented based on S/T instances; multi-cue parallelism is used to handle this variations. Hence, SMP-HMM is introduced to handle the segments and to train the lexicons constructed based on HS-HMM (Hand shape), TV-HMM (Temporal Velocity) and TP-HMM (Temporal Position).

3.6.2. *SU Training*

Based on Bakis topology, SMP-HMM is constructed with two states for T SUs and one state for S SUs. The Viterbi algorithm is engaged to train these HMM and to find the majority plausible state sequence in a repetitive manner. Once training is completed, parameters of HMM is estimated, i.e. the log likelihood of all the training data. This process is repeated until all the data are trained without further increase in likelihood of the HMM parameters. After this training, Baum-Welch algorithm is applied to re-calculate the parameter values for both spatial and temporal SUs. When all the training samples are processed, the total accumulative set of statistical values of HMM and temporal HMM is re-estimated.

3.6.3. *SU Recognition*

When the training is complete, sign instances need to be recognized based on the constructed subunit models. The subunit recognition is done based on the trained HMM along with the constructed SU lexicon. The recognition begins with each node in the HMM emits a state through the exact path for a test example t with T frames. All the path value has to be calculated and summed to find the individual transition log-probability and also the log-probability of emitting node. The most probable S/T sequence at each time instance is computed to maximize the above log-probability estimated from each path in the recognition network.

3.7. System Implementation

To recognize sign sentences and isolated words from continuous video sequences, the proposed approach introduces novel classification techniques namely BPaHMM and SMP-HMM based on some of the machine learning techniques which includes Hidden Markov Model, Minimum Entropy Clustering and Dynamic Time warping. The training sequences of images are obtained from the video in the resolution range of 195 X 165 pixels to 640 X 480 pixels.

The proposed approach is evaluated against three different benchmark sign language corpora which include ASLLVD (American Sign Language), RWTH-BOSTON-104 (British Sign Language) and RWTH-PHOENIX-Weather (German Sign Language). Also, the proposed approach is trained and tested with three different self-captured videos from the web camera, used in order to evaluate the efficiency of proposed approach against various illuminations and backgrounds. The dependencies of the proposed approach include OpenCV 2.4.1.1 using C# for image pre-processing and Scikit-Learn 0.18.1 for training the S/T Subunits using machine learning algorithms.

3.8. Summary

This chapter describes various components of the proposed subunit sign modelling framework to recognize large-vocabulary sign corpus. This chapter also depicts the overview of the elements of all the foremost components which constitute the major part in recognizing the sign language sentences. Also, the proposed system implementation based on computer vision and machine learning algorithms are discussed. The evaluation of the proposed approach based on training and testing sequences are also described.

CHAPTER IV

4. Extricating Manual and Non-Manual Features for Subunit Sign Modelling

4.1. Introduction

The selection and extraction of best features to recognize signs play a vital role in the performance of the system. Sign language is least consistent but more emblematic and more ordered among gesture classes. Extraction of features comprises numerous components like hand and arm gestures, head positions, face and facial expressions, lip movements and body postures. This set of feature groups makes the recognition of an isolated and continuous sequence of signs highly complex. Even though different proposals have been made, an automatic recognition of sign language still runs as an open research problem.

In this book, an automatic sign language recognition and classification system is proposed. This chapter focuses on subunit extraction and signer independent action recognition for large-vocabulary signs. In Subunit Extraction, the feature vectors are extracted based on both spatial and temporal feature groups to form the subunit gesture base. In this work, shape-based features and region-based features are considered as subunit-manual spatial feature vectors. At the same time, motion trajectories are estimated to form the subunit-manual temporal feature vectors. The facial parameters namely shape and texture information are extracted to structure the subunit-non-manual feature vectors. Extraction of manual and non-manual features using subunit modelling helps to resolve the movement ambiguity which is one of the most important issues in real world sign language recognition. Signer independent action aims in using a single web camera for different signer behaviour patterns and for cross-signer validation. The main advantage of the proposed work is the provision of a system for automatic recognition of sign language and to apply them to effective communication.

The proposed approach solves the two major issues faced by current SLR systems namely Feature Extraction and Selection and Cross-Signer Validation. A novel Bayesian Parallel Hidden Markov Model is introduced to classify the manual and non-manual cues. These cues have more than features for one sign; Parallel HMM is used for subunit extraction and to combine the features of manual and non-manual parameters to yield better results in classification and recognition of signs. This proposed BPaHMM combines the visual and linguistic transcriptions of sign lexicon along with extracted manual and non-manual features to form a subunit gesture base. Signer independent action aims in using a single web camera for different signer behaviour patterns and for cross-signer validation.

4.2. Architecture of Feature Extraction

The system overview of proposed subunit modelling for Feature Extraction of manual and non-manual cues is illustrated in figure 4.1. The schematic process of the proposed system follows three stages: Pre-Processing, Subunit Extraction, and classification. In the first step, image sequences are pre-processed by background subtraction followed by erosion and dilation process. In the second stage, the manual and non-manual features are extracted in parallel, based on subunits. The extracted features are clustered along with sign lexicon to form a subunit gesture base.

Before classification, an essential stage included in this work is pre-classification. This phase will eliminate the movement ambiguities between one sign and the other in the given sequence of signs. This step finds the movement ambiguities once the subunits are segmented, and also it reduces the processing time by reducing discriminative vocabularies and sharing subunits across feature vectors. Finally, manual and non-manual features are classified independently and combined to yield the sign recognition result. Further sections gives the details about the components involved in sign gesture recognition.

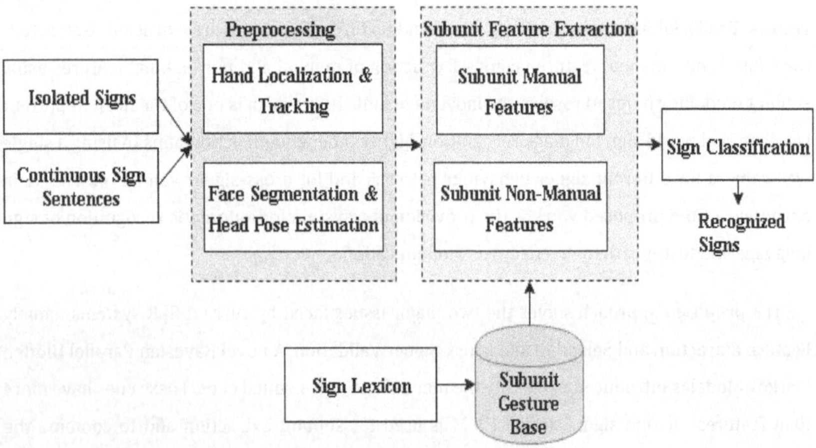

Figure 4.1: Architecture Overview of Proposed Manual and Non-manual Feature Extraction

4.2.1. *Pre-Processing*

Pre-Processing is the most essential part in recognizing the sign languages. It is responsible for processing the front videos and producing the extracted features for further processing of subunits. These features are going to serve as the input for subunit extraction. Hand and face localization and tracking are performed by identifying skin pixels in the area of interest. Hand tracking algorithm proposed is simple, efficient and also easy to understand so that it can be applied to real time applications. This algorithm is based on the colour detection and motion of the hand. The frames are converted into gray scale images, then a frame matching algorithm is used to analyse the movement of the hand direction. In this stage, the static background is subtracted in the dynamic video sequence.

Background subtraction is involved in two subsequent processes: Erosion and Dilation. Erosion process is used to reduce the noise in the frames of the unaided video sequence. Once the erosion is done, Dilation is used to manipulate the geographical area of the frames. Hand and face localization and tracking are performed by identifying skin pixels in the area of interest. After hand localization and tracking, the manual and non-manual features are extracted to represent the position and trajectories of hand with respect to the head position to locate the signs in given video sequences. The centroid coordinate of the frames is extracted with reference to head position to construct the feature groups of temporal subunits whereas the shape features are estimated based on Fourier transform to construct the spatial subunits. Finally, both the features are given as input to the Hidden Markov Model to classify the sign gestures.

4.2.2. *Subunit Feature Extraction*

Subunit extraction involves the sequential and parallel breakdown of sign gestures without any prior knowledge of syllables and the number of subunits. A novel Bayesian Parallel Hidden Markov Model is introduced for subunit extraction. This proposed BPaHMM combines the visual and linguistic transcriptions of sign lexicon along with extracted manual and non-manual features to form a subunit gesture base. The manual and non-manual features are extracted by using Parallel Hidden Markov Model. Manual feature groups are formed from the feature vectors of hand gestures. Similarly, non-manual feature groups are formed from the feature vectors of face postures. These feature vectors are sequentially segmented and simultaneously given as the input signals to Parallel HMM to classify the subunits. Based on the output state of PaHMM, a Bi-fold Bayesian network is constructed by merging the subunits from manual and non-manual feature groups to form subunit gesture base. Figure 4.2 shows the illustration of the construction of Bi-fold Bayesian Parallel Hidden Markov Model.

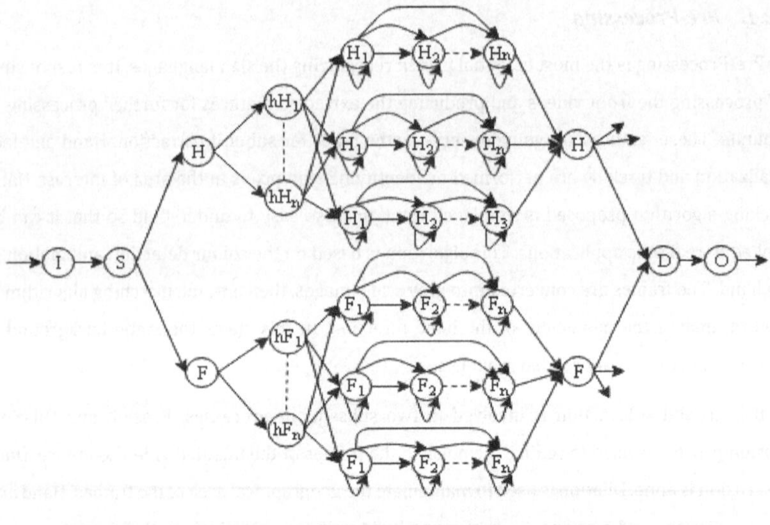

Figure 4.2: Illustration of Bi-fold Bayesian Parallel Hidden Markov Model

From figure 4.2, based on subjective logic of Bayesian model the notation is defined for the joint probability distribution. It is denoted as

$$P(\omega^{S}_{H\bar{|}F}) = \frac{P(\omega^{S}_{H|F})h(H)}{P(\omega^{S}_{F|H})h(H) + P(\omega^{S}_{F|\neg H})h(\neg H)} \quad (4.1)$$

where S denotes the sign sequence, H denotes the subunit manual features and F represents subunit non-manual features. The pair $(\omega^{S}_{F|H}, \omega^{S}_{F|\neg H})$ denotes the source S based on binomial conditional opinions and the argument h(H) denotes the prior probability of manual feature H. The pair $(\omega^{S}_{H\bar{|}F}, \omega^{S}_{H\bar{|}\neg F})$ denotes inverted conditional opinions and $(\omega^{S}_{H|F})$ denotes the conditional opinion that generalizes the probabilistic condition $P(H \mid F)$.

Once the sign sequence is performed by the signer, the system identifies the localization of hand and face in the sequence of frames before extracting the features from the sign gestures. The Bi-fold Bayesian network segments and forwards the extracted segment to the first layer as manual features and for the second layer, it forwards the non-manual features. Parallel Hidden Markov Model handles parallel signals with sequential segmentation of subunits. Each signal consists of the sequence of subunits each with one feature vector. General notations for HMM based on Viterbi algorithm is given as

$$P(Q,O/\lambda)=\max\{\delta t(i)\} \tag{4.2}$$

where $\delta t(i)=\max P(Q_1,Q_2,\ldots Q_t=S_i,\ O/\lambda)$ (4.3)

where Si represents a number of states, Q denotes the input state sequence, O represents output sequence, and λ represents hyper-parameter. The parallel HMMs is defined ass

$$Q_{1\ldots c}(\sum_{j=1}^{w}\sum_{i=1}^{c} w_{ji}.\log p(Q_{ij},O_{ji}\mid\lambda)) \tag{4.4}$$

where $\sum_{i}$. wji represents the segment weights for a word j in channel i. The proposed BPaHMM handles both manual and non-manual features to form a single subunit. It is calculated as

$$Q_{1\ldots c}(\sum_{j=1}^{w}\sum_{i=1}^{c} w_{ji}.\log p(Q_{ij},O_{ji}\mid\lambda_{manual}).\sum_{j=1}^{w}\sum_{i=1}^{c} w_{ji}.\log p(Q_{ij},O_{ji}\mid\lambda_{non-manual})) \tag{4.5}$$

One interesting fact in the proposed system is the construction of intra-gloss sign lexicon. After segmenting and modelling the subunits, different signs of similar features share their subunits by calculating the corresponding feature vector, that is, two signs having same hand shape but different hand motion will share the shape subunits in gesture base.

Let us assume Y_{ji} is the subunit for the word j in channel i with similar features of another word X_{ij}. To find subunit sharing, the dominant features of both the words are extracted, based on strong signal $h(x_i|j)$. It is denoted as

$$h(x_i\mid j)=\frac{\sum_i W_i Y_{ij}}{\sum_i W_{ij}} \tag{4.6}$$

After calculating this strong signal, it is included in the Parallel HMM state sequence to share the subunits of similar class. Hence the subunit sharing equation is written as

$$Q_{1\ldots c}\sum_{j=1}^{c}(\sum_{j=1}^{w}\sum_{i=1}^{c} wji.\log p(Qij,Oji|\lambda manual).\sum_{j=1}^{w}\sum_{i=1}^{c} wji.\log p(Qij,Oji|\lambda non\text{-}manual)).(Y_{ji}|h(\mathbf{x}_i,j)) \tag{4.7}$$

where Y_{ji} is the subunits with similar features and $h(x_i,j)$ is strong signal constructed from the shared features and weak hand signals.

4.2.2.1. Subunit Manual Feature Extraction

Manual feature groups are constructed by the breaking down of hand signals and sign sequence into subunits without any prior information about knowledge source like the movement-hold model. In fact, a subunit is represented by a feature group with different feature vectors. In the proposed system, the spatiotemporal features for hand signals are considered and it is illustrated in figure 4.3.

Subunit spatial features are derived from shape based and region based information. In this work, the shape-based features namely Fourier descriptors and curvature representors are considered whereas, for the region-based features, moments and moment-based invariants are considered. All these features together form the subunit spatial feature vectors.

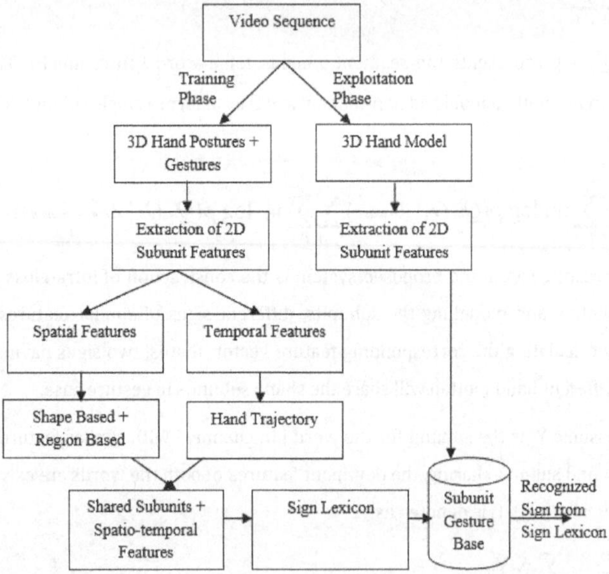

Figure 4.3 Subunit Manual Features Extraction

Unlike movement-hold model, no prior information about the gesture knowledge is available except the sign sequence. So, it is mandatory to consider the temporal feature group to construct the subunit manual features. Hand trajectory analysis is considered as the unique attribute for selection of temporal features. Hand shape is estimated using the Fourier Descriptors (FD). Fourier Descriptors are calculated on the contour of the hand region. Complex coordinates are used, each point P_i of the shape contour is represented by a complex number z_i, with N the number of points of the contour:

$$P_i(x_i, y_i) \Leftrightarrow z_i = x_i + jy_i,\ i = 1, \ldots N-1 \qquad (4.8)$$

Where x_i and y_i are the horizontal and vertical position coordinates of each of the N boundary points.

Hand contour is sampled to obtain a normalized contour length before calculating the FD using Discrete Fourier series. Sampling is done by calculating interpolation points of an equal arc length. Here, the length of an arc has been chosen to satisfy the hand shape description and smoothening of the hand shape without any sharp edges or noise. Also for the computational efficiency the number of interpolating boundary points has been chosen to be power of 2 and the normalized length is chosen as N=64 points. Hence the Fourier Transform leads to N Fourier coefficients Z_k. It is represented in Fourier series as

$$Z_k = \sum_{i=0}^{N-1} e^{(\frac{-2\pi jkn}{N})} Z_i, \forall k \in [0, N-1] \tag{4.9}$$

Where k represents the coefficients of the Fourier descriptors such as Z_0, Z_1, etc. until it reaches the shape of N boundary points and n varies up to N-1 points.

Here, the first coefficient Z_0 is discarded due to the presence of translation information (only position) of the hand shape. Similarly, rotation invariance, scale invariance and starting point invariance are also calculated because all these have greater influence in affecting the shape information. Rotation invariance of the FD is attained by taking the magnitude of coefficients; scale invariance is attained by dividing coefficients with the magnitude of the second coefficient, Z_1 and starting point invariance is attained by taking only the magnitude of the Fourier descriptors. Finally, N -2 Fourier descriptors M_k is obtained:

$$M_k = \frac{|Z_k|}{|Z_1|}, k = 2,..N-1 \tag{4.10}$$

From figure 4.4, it is clearly noted that the hand contour can be well constructed using 20 coefficients but to eliminate noise and get the smoothening appearance, the proposed approach used 64 boundary points to extract hand shape. Also it can be seen that the hand shape is contoured for different skin tone under different illuminations.

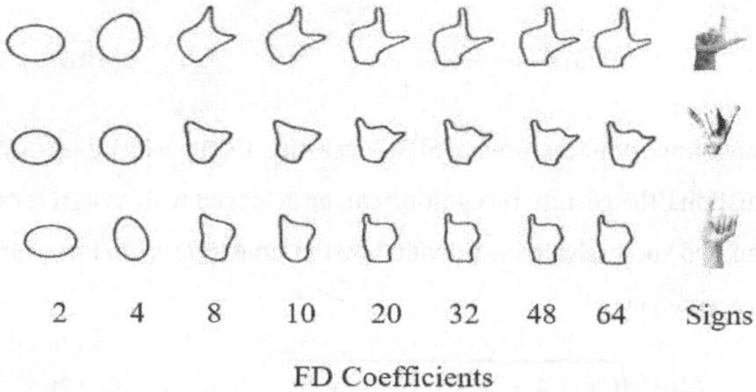

Figure 4.4: Construction of Hand Shape Using FD Coefficients

Hand trajectory information is represented on the basis of six feature vectors. Let us consider, the hand trajectory (HT) consisting of Cartesian coordinates (x_i, y_i), i=1,2,....k where (x_i,y_i) represents the location of the hand in the kth frame and (x_{k+1}, y_{k+1}) represents the coordinates of next frame. The occurrence of the first position of the hand is computed as the Euclidean distance between the starting point of the hands and centroid (x_c,y_c) of the trajectory. These notations are similarly applicable for the equations from eqn.4.11 to eqn.4.22.

$$H_{pos1} = \sqrt{(x_{k+1} - x_c)^2 + (y_{k+1} - y_c)^2} \tag{4.11}$$

Where (x_c,y_c) is computed after each frame, it is denoted by

$$(x_c, y_c) = \sum_{i=1}^{k} \frac{x_i}{k} . \sum_{i=1}^{k} \frac{y_i}{k} \tag{4.12}$$

The occurrence of the second position of hand coordinates in the trajectory is estimated as the distance between the starting point of the hand gesture and the current point of the hand gesture in the next frame. It is represented as

$$H_{pos2} = \sqrt{(x_{k+1} - x_1)^2 + (y_{k+1} - y_1)^2} \tag{4.13}$$

The next feature considered is hand orientation. It is computed based on the hand displacement vector at each frame according to the centroid of the hand trajectory.

$$O_c = \arctan \frac{y_{k+1} - y_c}{x_{k+1} - x_c} \tag{4.14}$$

Hand orientation between two successive frames is computed as

$$O_s = \arctan \frac{y_{k+1} - y_k}{x_{k+1} - x_k} \tag{4.15}$$

Hand orientation between starting point and current point in the trajectory is calculated as

$$O_g = \arctan \frac{y_{k+1} - y_1}{x_{k+1} - x_1} \tag{4.16}$$

One of the most important features of SLR is velocity. Using velocity feature vector during some critical situations, the gesture recognition can be achieved with ease. It is calculated as the distance between two successive points divided by the time interval in terms of the number of frames. It is represented by

$$H_v = \sqrt{(x_{k+1} - x_k)^2 + (y_{k+1} - y_k)^2} \tag{4.17}$$

Finally, subunit manual feature extraction group is extracted from the Cartesian coordinate system. The feature vector at frame k+1 is obtained by the union of Z_k, H_{pos1}, H_{pos2}, O_c, O_s, O_g, H_v. The first feature vector denotes spatial features whereas the rest six represents the temporal features. Figure 4.5a and figure 4.5b show the identification of manual subunit features and recognition of signs from continuous video sequences in real-time environment.

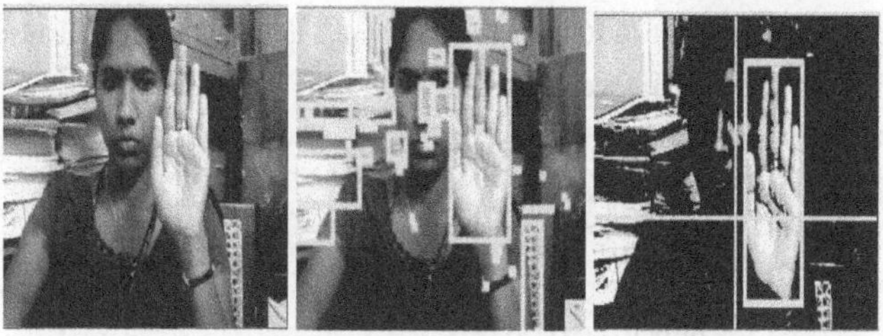

Figure 4.5a: Subunit Manual Features Extraction in Real-Time Environment

Figure 4.5b: Subunit Manual Sign Recognition in Real-Time Environment

4.2.2.2. *Subunit Non-Manual Feature Extraction*

Non-manual feature groups are generally constructed from the feature vectors of upper body posture. In sign language recognition, certain signs are similar according to its manual gesture and such signs can be identified only with the help of non-manual parameters. The PaHMM model for non-manual feature vector is constructed in such a way that each feature vector represents one subunit.

The essential feature vectors to construct the non-manual features are face shape and head pose estimation. The detailed representation of skin tone identification is done based on enhanced peer model using vector distance. Initially, it is assumed as pixel=[RGB] where R=0, G=255 and b=0 if the searching pixel is a green vector and it is set as reference colour and changed to HSV values. The vector distance between the pixels are computed as

$$D = \sqrt{(R-0)^2 + (G-255)^2 + (B-0)^2} \quad (4.18)$$

The enhancement of the peer model with normalization is designed to get the average skin colour of the people from various racial majorities, and also under different lighting conditions giving better results. This enhanced peer model is represented with the following values and conditions. The values of RGB is set to the threshold such that R>95, G>40 and B>20. Also, Max(R,G,B)-Min(R,G,B)>15 Abs(R-G)>15 with R>G, R>B and G>B. Based on the histogram, the conversion of RGB to HSV space is done as

$$H = \arccos \frac{\frac{1}{2}((R-G)+(R-B))}{\sqrt{(R-G)^2+(R-B)(G-B)}} \quad (4.19)$$

$$S = 1 - 3\frac{\min(R,G,B)}{R+G+B} \quad (4.20)$$

$$V = \frac{1}{3}(R+G+B) \quad (4.21)$$

Finally, the HSV values are set to H<=19, S>=48 and V>35. Using the listed steps, the face shape can be segregated from the given set of pixels. Head pose is estimated by using Principal Component Analysis, the component will transform the face region into Eigen values.

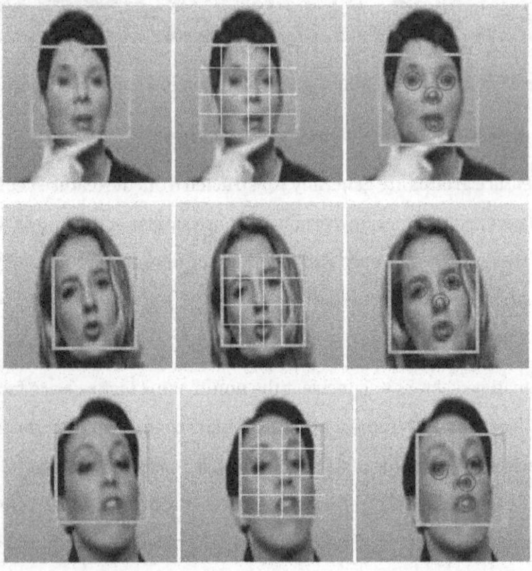

Figure 4.6: Subunit Non-Manual Feature Extraction in RWTH-PHOENIX-Weather Dataset

Eigen values represented in terms of different poses ranging from -60o to +60o by rotating the head position. Distance between the head position and the hand in k[th] frame is calculated as

$$HH = \sqrt{(x_h - x_k)^2 + (y_h - y_k)^2} \tag{4.22}$$

Where (x_h, y_h) represents head coordinates in the current frame and (x_k, y_k) represents the hand coordinates. Figure 4.6 illustrates the extraction of non-manual signs from the continuous video sequences with the head position ranging from -60° to +60°.

4.2.3. *Combination of Combined Probabilities*

The corresponding combined probability for one subunit is represented as

$$P(o \mid \lambda) = P(o \mid \lambda_{manual}).P(o \mid \lambda_{non-manual}) \tag{4.23}$$

Where $P(O / \lambda_{manual})$ represents subunit manual feature groups denoted as $Q_1.....Q_c\{P(O \mid \lambda_{shape}).P(O \mid \lambda_{curvature}).P(O \mid \lambda_{position}).P(O \mid \lambda_{orientation}).P(O \mid \lambda_{motionspeed})\}$ and $P(O \mid \lambda_{non-manual})$ represents subunit non-manual feature groups represented as $Q_1.....Q_c\{P(O \mid \lambda_{faceshape}).P(O \mid \lambda_{headposition})\}$. Using Bayesian rule, the highest probability of subunit is chosen as

$$P(\lambda_{manual} \mid \lambda_{nonmanual}) = \frac{P(\lambda_{nonmanual} \mid \lambda_{manual})\, P(\lambda_{manual})}{P(\lambda_{nonmanual})} \tag{4.24}$$

Based on Bakis topology, the subunit gesture base is constructed as shown in figure 4.7.

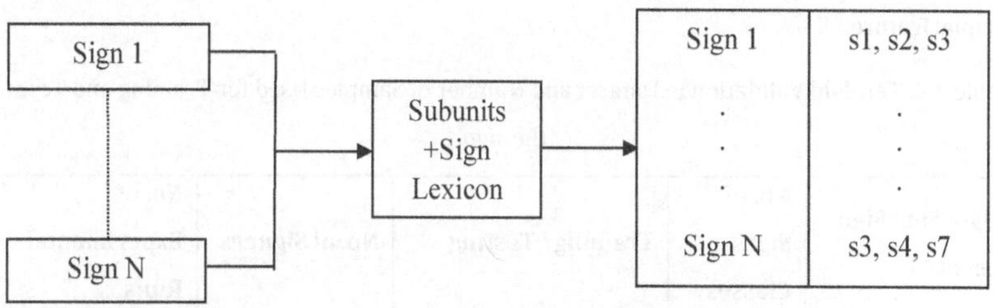

Figure 4.7: Representation of Construction of Subunit Gesture Base

4.3. Result Analysis and Discussions

The proposed ASLCR system extracts the features using OpenCV and learned the Bayesian Classifier to classify manual and non-manual features with Scikit-learn. The proposed BPaHMM is evaluated subjectively and quantitatively with real time signing videos. These videos were gathered from different resources: one data source (Neidle et al. 2012) namely ASLLVD was kindly provided by Vassilis Athitsos collected at Boston University, and it is publically available at http: // secrets. rutgus. edu/ dai/ querypages/ search/ search.php. It consists of isolated and compound signs. Second dataset consists of self-captured sign video which comprise of isolated signs and signs from RWTH-Boston-104 database consisting of continuous sequences. The summary of experimental data set and validation methods are indicated in table 4.1 and table 4.2.

Table 4.1: Summary of Dataset Used in Evaluation

Data Set/ Sign Level	**No. of Signers**	**No. of Video instances**	**No. of Signs**	**Video Resolution**	**Key Frames/ Second**
ASLLVD- Isolated	6	9800	3300	195 X 165 Pixels	30
RWTH-BOSTON-104- Continuous	3	201	104	195 X 165 Pixels	30

4.3.1. Analysis of Extracted Features

The efficiency of different features is analysed first to find the importance of each feature (subunit) in recognizing the sign gestures. In this research work, extraction of seven essential features has been discussed. Seven aspects of features namely Z_K, H_{pos1}, H_{pos2}, O_c, O_s, O_g, and H_V to characterize the spatial and temporal aspects of manual features. Similarly, one aspect of HH feature is extracted to characterize the position of the head to hand temporal aspect of the non-manual feature.

Table 4.2: Ten-fold Validation in Dataset and Number of Samples Used for Training and Testing the signs

Data Set/ Sign Level	**No. of Sign Classes**	**Training/ Testing**	**No. of Signers**	**No. of Experimental Runs**
ASLLVD- Isolated	33	2:18 (Per 20 samples of each sign Class with repetition of two signer videos)	Two Signers for Training and one for Testing	10 repetitions
RWTH- BOSTON-104- Continuous	10			

These entire eight features make the recognition becomes tedious. To indicate the importance of each feature involved recognition need to be estimated based on the information gain. To estimate the feature importance, the experiment was run repeatedly ten times for each sign class to construct lexicon. Based on the experiments the number of subunits for each sign class is adjusted. Table 4.3 lists the importance of each feature in the sign classes.

Table 4.3: Importance of Feature Extrication

No. of Sign Classes	Z_K %	H_{pos1} %	H_{pos2} %	O_c %	O_s %	O_g %	HV %	HH %
1	29.70	4.30	3.60	5.30	3.40	2.90	28.30	22.50
2	31.20	4.40	4.70	7.20	5.40	2.60	25.40	19.10
3	33.10	3.30	1.50	2.20	7.30	2.70	26.30	23.60
4	24.10	6.10	5.20	3.40	3.20	1.10	31.20	25.70
5	27.80	2.10	4.80	1.50	2.10	5.50	33.70	21.50

From table 4.3, it is noted that the first feature Z_K and the last two features H_V and HH are likely to have more information gain when compared with other five features. Therefore, it is concluded that one spatial feature that is the hand shape and two temporal features namely hand velocity and position of the hand trajectory from head to hand are considered to be the most essential features amongst all other features because these three features occupy almost 25 percent to 30 percent in each sign classes, where as the rest occupies up to 1 percent to 5 percent. The recognition and classification of signs now becomes more feasible and quicker since the number of feature class comparison in the gesture base is less.

4.3.1.1. Feature Combinations

The efficacy of multiple features and their combinations is evaluated to find the most prompting feature combination and to improve the efficiency of the recognition rate. First, the estimation is done on the individual features and then several combinations of the selected features from section 4.4.1 are tested and the results are evaluated. RWTH-BOSTON-104 has been used to test the feature combinations. In this data set, three signers performed the sign actions of 201 continuous sentences. The experiment was carried out for 30 isolated words from ASLLVD and 110 utterances of continuous sentences from RWTH-BOSTON-104.

The number of utterances used for training is 30 and for testing the remaining 110 samples have been used. The video frames are collected in the range of 30 key frames per second and the size of the single frame used in the recognition is 195 X 165 pixels. Table 4.4 shows the correctly classified utterances and misclassified utterances when considering individual features, the combination of one or more features and the combination of all the features. Among the performance of the individual features, hand shape feature gives the least error rate of 8.57% from table 4.4.

Table 4.4: Importance of Feature Combinations

Features & its Combinations	# Correctly Classified Utterances	# Misclassified Utterances	Error Rate (%)
Z_K	128	12	8.57
H_V	126	14	10.00
HH	123	17	12.14
Z_K + H_V	131	9	6.42
Z_K + HH	129	11	7.86
H_V + HH	121	19	13.57
Z_K + H_V + HH	135	5	3.57

Also, when the hand shape is combined with velocity and position the error rate is reduced to 2.15% and 0.71%, that is, the error rate is reduced when it combines with velocity. Similarly, when all three features are combined together, the error rate is reduced to 3.57%.

Therefore, based on the analysis done in section 4.4.1 and the results obtained in section 4.4.1.1, it is proved that with the help of hand shape, position and velocity, the proposed feature combination can achieve better recognition. These results are plotted as a graph in figure 4.8.

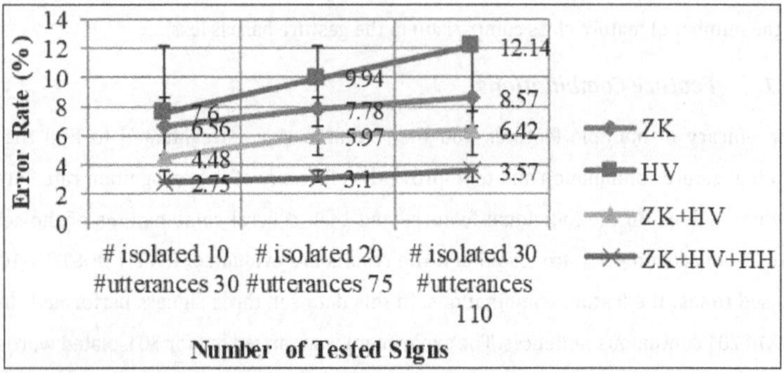

Figure 4.8: Different Feature Combinations and Error Rate Estimation

4.3.2. Evaluation of Subunit Segmentation

In the experimental runs, a different amount of arbitrarily selected training samples in the sort of 1 to 10 is used, and the remaining samples are used for testing. Based on the segmented subunits, the experiments were conducted five times, and the mean results were documented.

Two metrics namely recall, and precision are used to measure the performance. The average comparison result is listed in table 4.5 and table 4.6 for isolated and continuous signs respectively.

$$Recall = \frac{No.\ of\ correctly\ classified\ subunits\ (CS)}{No.\ Of\ original\ subunits\ in\ gesture\ base\ (OS)} \tag{4.25}$$

$$Precision = \frac{No.\ of\ correctly\ classified\ subunits\ (CS)}{No.\ Of\ detected\ subunits\ (DS)} \tag{4.26}$$

Once the sign sequence from the camera is given as input to PaHMMs, the model constructed in figure 4.9 explains the elimination of movement ambiguities using subunit model. Since the subunits are formed by the 8-dimensional feature vectors, the PaHMMs are built with 8-channels.

Table 4.5: Performance of Subunit Extraction for Isolated Signs

S. No	Sign	OS	DS	CS	Recall	Precision
1	Advise	1	1	1	1	1
2	Cold	3	4	2	0.67	0.75
3	Blood	2	3	2	1	1
4	Accident	3	3	3	1	1
5	Blind	2	2	2	1	1
Average					**0.934**	**0.884**

Table 4.6: Performance of Subunit Extraction for Continuous Sign Sequences

S. No	Sign	OS	DS	CS	Recall	Precision
1	Need + Water	9	13	8	0.88	0.62
2	Are + you + studying	17	19	15	0.88	0.79
3	She +is+ teaching	11	15	11	1	0.73
4	I +want+ to +claim +up	23	24	21	0.91	0.87
5	Brother + and +sister	17	19	15	0.88	0.79
Average					**0.91**	**0.76**

In figure 4.9, at the time interval t8, none of the feature vectors emits probability. Similarly, after t4, the output sequence does not reflect any subunit similarity features. Therefore, it can be concluded that without any explicit modelling for movement ambiguities, it is eliminated directly during exploitation.

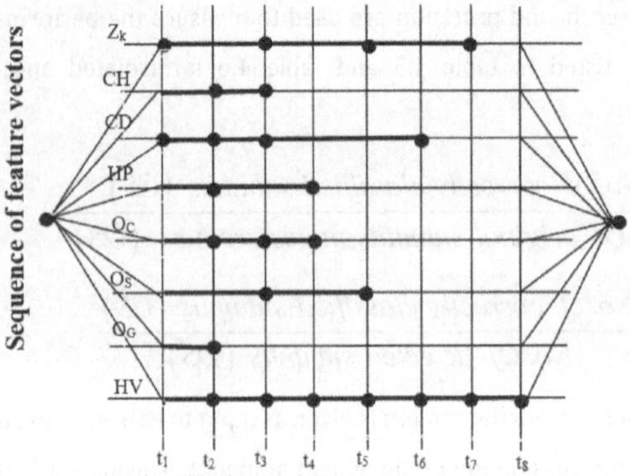

t1...t8 is the time steps of the consecutive frames

Figure 4.9: Sign "GOOD" Subunit Segmentation

4.3.3. Evaluation of Subunit Sharing

One of the key features of the proposed work is the subunit feature vector sharing among the subunit classes in sign lexicon to reduce the vocabulary size and processing time of the proposed system. The sharing of subunits for the signs "like" and "taste" is represented in figure 4.10. In this figure, segmentation of similar subunits for different signs according to the features is shown.

These two different signs have shared the subunits because of its similar feature vectors. In the temporal frame ranging between 60 and 90, the signs have similar feature vectors and so while constructing the sign lexicon shared subunits are stored only once. Whenever it is needed for recognition, it will be retrieved for both the signs. Thus, for the large vocabulary of signs, there is no need to construct the sign lexicon for explicit movement subunits.

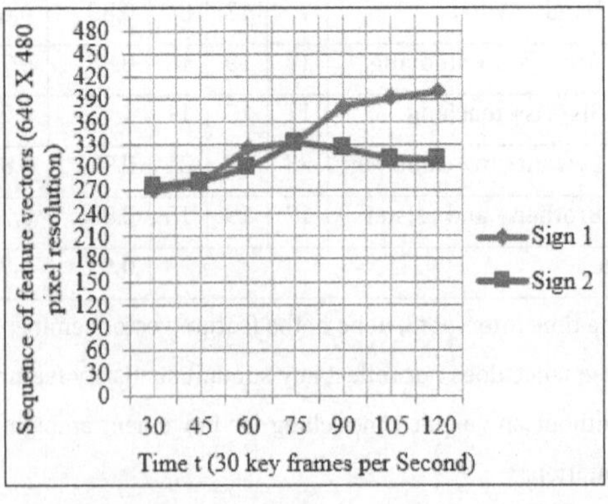

Figure 4.10: Subunit Sharing Between "Like" and "Taste" Signs

4.3.4. *Evaluation of Subunit Modelling and Whole Sign Modelling*

Performance evaluation of subunit model is carried on RWTH-Boston 104 continuous sign sequence and ASLLVD isolated signs. The automated transcriptions of signs into subunits are presented in section 2 are used. Sign lexicon was constructed for 50 isolated signs and 100 continuous sign sentences, and the remaining samples were used for testing. Subsequently, the random selection was made based on the ten repetitions of 5 isolated signs and 30 continuous sequences of signs. Totally, 400 video sequences were collected to perform the evaluation. The evaluation of this experiment was carried out in two ways. The first assessment was done for the classification of isolated signs and second evaluation was done for the classification of continuous signs. The results obtained are comparatively estimated with work done by (Fang et al. 2004, Cooper et al. 2010) and the results are plotted in figure 4.11.

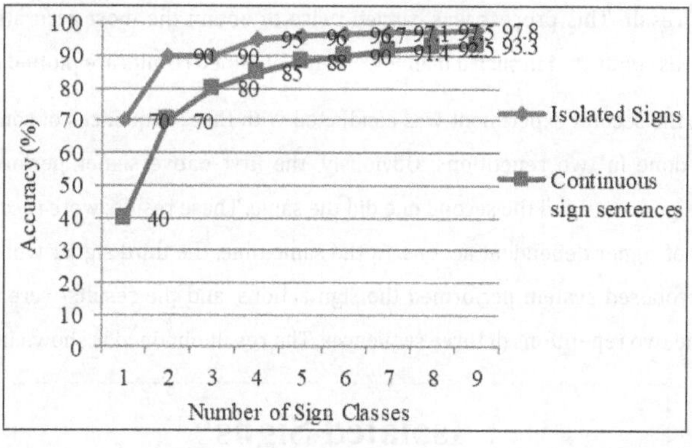

Figure 4.11: Performance of Subunit Modelling for Isolated and Continuous Signs

From the dataset, for recognizing isolated signs totally 100 sample videos were collected. For each sign, ten samples of videos consisting of one positive sample, and nine negative samples were chosen for training the isolated signs. Similarly, the system was trained for all signs, and the rest of the videos were used for testing. As reported for isolated signs, training, and testing were conducted to recognize the continuous video sequences. Three hundred video samples were considered for continuous sign sentences by way of collecting ten repetitions of 30 sign sequences. For training, for each sentence one positive video sample and 29 negative video samples were chosen. This process continued till it reached ten positive and 280 negative video samples and the remaining ten videos of samples were used to test the system.

From figure 4.11, it is clearly noted that the proposed BPaHMM for subunit modelling of sign language recognition shows an average of 97.8% accuracy. When compared with other existing works (Kruger et al. 2008, Cooper et al. 2010) it shows a variation of 18.6%. And it shows 0.2% accuracy when compared with (Li et al. 2015), and the authors have selected the training samples in the ratio of 1:19 whereas, the proposed approach has chosen the sample in the ratio of 1:9 for isolated signs. Similarly, when compared with (Han et al. 2013) the proposed BPaHMM shows almost 9% improvements in recognizing continuous sign sentences.

4.3.5. Evaluation and Analysis of Signer Action

Based on three experiments conducted in the above sections, the signer action estimation was carried out in such a way that two signers were used to do the actions and one signer was used for testing. The evaluation of signer action was performed in two subsequent experiments. In the first experiment, three sequences of isolated signs were done in two repetitions i.e. in detail, two native signers performed one sign action and another signer did the same action again to test result. This process was carried twice to obtain the most accurate results. The experiment was conducted in such a manner, and the obtained results are plotted in figure 4.12.

Similarly, the second experiment was conducted with three sequences of continuous signs which were done in two repetitions. Obviously, the first native signer performed the first sequence of signs twice and the second one did the same. These results were recorded to check the accuracy of signer dependent actions. At the same time, the third signer who was used for testing the proposed system performed the sign actions, and the results were concluded by combining the two repetitions of three sequences. The result obtained is shown in figure 4.13.

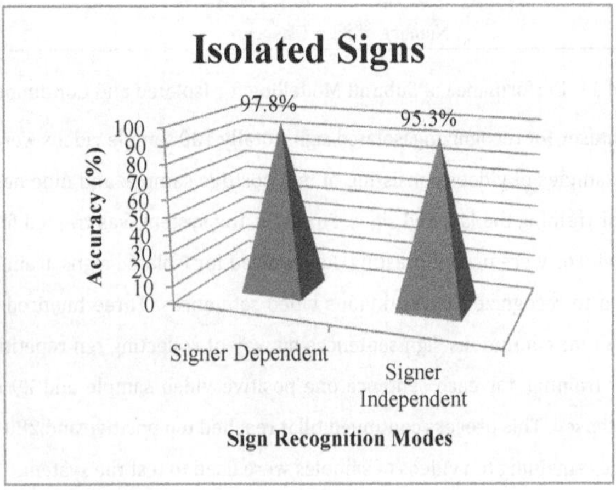

Figure 4.12: Cross-Signer Validation for Isolated Signs

From the figure 4.12 and figure 4.13, the signer dependent and independent actions are analyzed thoroughly based on the Precision and Recall metrics. The result shows that the proposed system recognizes 97.8% isolated signs and 93.3% continuous signs for signer dependent actions whereas for independent signer operations, the system recognizes 95.3% isolated signs and 82.1 % continuous sign sentences.

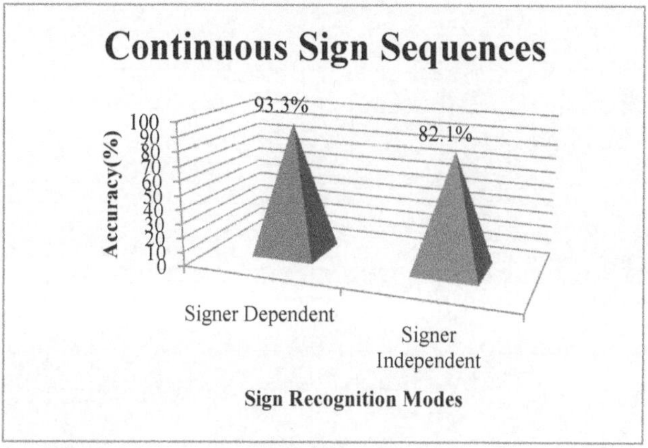

Figure 4.13: Cross-Signer Validations for Continuous Sign Sentences

4.4. Summary

This proposed work has made a tremendous contribution towards computer vision based sign language classification and recognition problems in subunit level. The proposed ASLCR system aims in solving the issues related to signer independent action and other relevant issues in feature extrication. Sophisticated techniques have been introduced and implemented to extort subunit based manual and non-manual features in the cluttered environment. A novel BPaHMM is introduced to classify the manual and non-manual cues and with the help of Parallel HMM, the manual and non-manual subunits are extracted successfully. Subunit gesture base formed with the help of these features allow the extension of vocabulary even without the training data by using the shared subunit feature. A discriminative feature selection is used to identify the importance of all selected and extracted features. Based on the feature selection, it is identified that the three useful subunits, hand shape, velocity and position are enough to be classified as subunits. Experimental results in four different dimensions have proved that the proposed ASLCR is efficient enough to adapt the real world constraints and it is scalable and reliable even for more number of vocabularies.

CHAPTER V

5. Subunit Modelling to Handle Epentheses Movements and Recognition Ambiguities in Sign Language

5.1. Introduction

In this research work, the problem of hand segmentation ambiguities and segregating epentheses movements between two adjacent signs in continuous video sequences are addressed. A novel subunit sign modelling framework is presented and illustrated to embark upon these problems while considering large-vocabularies. This framework is developed using a novel methodology of Enhanced Dynamic Programming (EDP) approach in subunit sign modelling. This EDP framework works with a combination of dynamic time warping and spatiotemporal clustering techniques.

Since, sign language consists of both spatial and temporal feature vectors, dynamic time warping is used as a measure of distance to compute the distance between two adjacent signs in sign trajectories. This distance is used as a temporal feature vector during the clustering of spatial feature vectors using MEC. This process is done recursively to cluster all the epentheses movements dynamically without using any explicit or implicit modelling. Experimental results have confirmed that the computation cost of the proposed system is less because the epenthesis movements are eliminated before classification and the gesture base space utilized by the sign gestures is very low because the proposed system does not require any modelling to handle epenthesis movements. The results obtained from the proposed subunit sign modelling framework is compared with other existing models in order to prove that the proposed system is best among the existing systems.

5.2. Background and Motivation

The major challenges that the current SLR systems face now are handling the large sign vocabularies in continuous video sequences. While recognizing signs from the continuous video, the present recognition methodologies struggle to identify and eliminate epentheses movements from sign actions, that is, to differentiate the gestures of signs rather than differentiating the movements that happened in between the signs.

Due to the presence of these extra movements, it is highly complicated for the present systems to identify and differentiate these movements from sign lexicons and it also affects the performance of the adjacent signs. Therefore, direct modelling of movement epentheses becomes a major problem while considering large vocabulary signs, and when these movements are left unconsidered, it creates the segmentation ambiguities during classification of sign gestures.

This proposed research work focuses on solving segmentation ambiguities of epentheses movement by adapting a framework based on the Enhanced Dynamic Programming approach in subunit sign modelling. Epentheses movements are associated with the ending state of the ancestor sign and starting state of the descendent state. However, it is very difficult in large vocabulary signs to obtain the frames of the starting and ending state of each sign. When it is segmented and annotated manually, there may be chances for the occurrence of man-made errors and it increases the huge ground work. Explicit or implicit modelling and manual annotations of epentheses movements lead to the recognition an infeasible task.

The Enhanced Dynamic Programming (EDP) approach presented in this book, sorts out the problem of hand gesture segmentation and epentheses movement ambiguities. This proposed EDP approach is an iterative approach based on spatiotemporal clustering and dynamic time warping. As epentheses movements are based on time-series features, spatial clustering alone will not be enough to handle temporal data. Dynamic time warping is adapted to handle such temporal features in sign language. To avoid clumsiness during training, the sign gestures alone are trained and stored in the gesture database whereas the epentheses movements are repetitively clustered and removed dynamically during testing.

5.3. Subunit Modelling Framework for Handling Epentheses Movements

The major components involved in this framework are Feature Extraction, Subunit Modelling, EDP iteration Process and Sign Classification. Extraction of sign features is the first stage in this proposed framework which involves collecting both manual and non-manual features of an individual sign in the continuous sign sentence video. These features are treated as subunits of an individual sign which will be given as an input while modelling the subunits. Subunit modelling is designed to concentrate on feature extraction of signs based on subunits and these extracted subunits are given as inputs to the modelling phase to classify the whole signs from associated epentheses movements.

The second element presented in this framework is the most essential component that involves neglecting the epentheses movements while the signer is performing the sign sequence. Yang et al. 2010 used the Dynamic Programming approach along with the enhanced level building algorithm used to find matching scores of manually labelled epentheses movements.

Since epentheses movements are present in the last frame of the preceding sign and the first frame of the following sign, without any explicit or implicit modelling it is difficult to predict such movements only by using the dynamic programming approach. Hence, the proposed approach enhanced the dynamic programming approach by using the clustering technique.

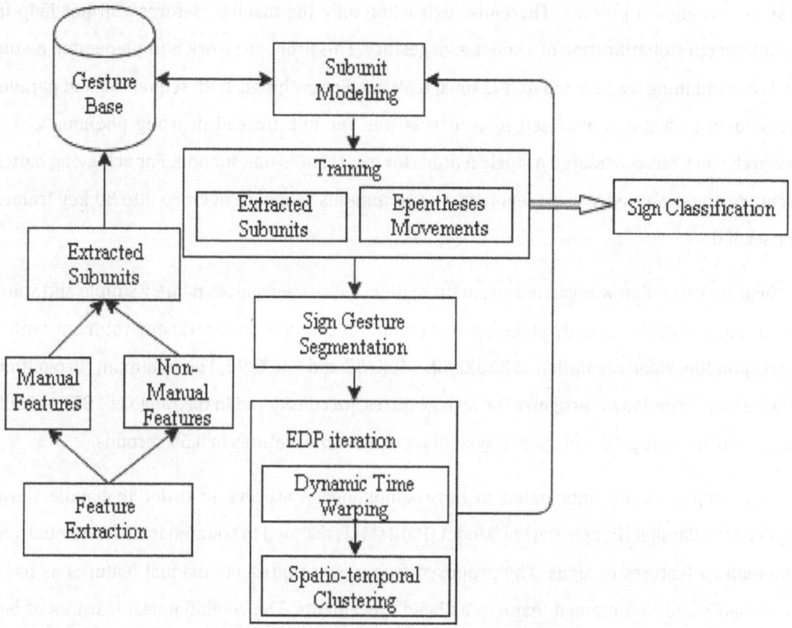

Figure 5.1: Proposed Subunit EDP Framework for Handling Epentheses Movements

This research work mainly concentrates on handling epentheses movements between adjacent signs; clustering only the spatial features will result in poor classification of sign gestures. To make effective classification and segmentation of sign gestures, temporal features are also considered while clustering. These temporal series of signs are calculated using the dynamic time warping technique as a distance measure between the two adjacent signs. This clustering process is done iteratively to remove all the epentheses movement and this process is named as the EDP iteration since it adapts the features of dynamic programming and spatiotemporal clustering. Finally, a sign classification component is used to separate the signs. The achievement in obtaining the clustered epentheses movements and its recursive actions are explained in detail in the following sections. Figure 5.1 illustrates the structure of the subunit sign modelling framework.

5.3.1. *Feature Extraction*

Generally, feature extraction is considered a most essential component in sign gesture recognition since this serves as the first stage behind all successful recognition processes. Sign language is considered to be the most structured when compared with the speech, text or gesture recognition process. Therefore, extracting only the manual features will not help in completing the identification of a single sign gesture. This proposed work is implemented on the basis of combining manual and non-manual features. For each sign, both sequential and parallel breakdown of features are used to construct one subunit. Instead of using phonemes, this research work has considered a single feature for each sign as one subunit. For achieving better accuracy, the proposed system segments the continuous sequence of video into 30 key frames per second.

Feature extraction was carried out in three different circumstances namely simple and static background, complex and dynamic environment and complex and static environment with a corresponding video resolution of 320X240, 640X480 and 640X290. The minimum recognition and resolution points to recognize the sign gestures are considered in the range of 1875 ~ 7500 points. On an average, the proposed system recognizes the features in 0.59 seconds.

Sign languages are anticipated to have simultaneous aspects. In order to handle those aspects, the Parallel Hidden Markov Model (PaHMM) is adopted to countenance the manual and non-manual features of signs. The proposed framework represents manual features as hand movements and non-manual features as head movements. The combinatorial features of left hand, right hand and head are used to form a subunit gesture base. Since signs follow the parallel usage of both the hands and head movements, channelizing these features in single stream PaHMM is infeasible and not much efficient for classification and recognition.

To channelize the subunit, Multi-stream PaHMM is introduced in this framework. The subunits are formed from the features namely hand shape, hand position, hand orientation, velocity and head position. These subunits are channelized via each stream in multi-stream in such a way that one channel of PaHMM is framed for one feature vector. The major concern in extracting the features is tracing the boundaries because the epentheses movements are present in between the adjacent frames of consecutive signs. Algorithm 5.1 lists the steps involved in tracing the trajectories of hand boundaries.

Initially, let us assume that the range of the coordinates for the search region in the window is (x,y). The following algorithm 4.1 calculates the bounding box of the hand gestures.

Algorithm 5.1 Tracing of Boundary around the Hand Gesture

Step1: Initialize the search window w, with the range (x,y) that is, the size of the window.

Step2: Calculate the base region b(x,y) of the hand gestures detected in the frames.

Step3: Calculate the centroid c(xc,yc) of the window.

Step4: Calculate the diameter d, with the estimated centroids to find the length l(x,y).

$$l(x,y) = 2 * c(xc, yc) \quad (5.1)$$

Step5: Let k be the constant vector added to the breadth w(x,y) to form the bounding box BB(x,y).

$$W(x,y) = 2k + b(x,y) \quad (5.2)$$

Step6: Search window w1 is constructed and the bounding for the meaningful gesture is calculated from equation 1 and equation 2 as

$$BB(x,y) = 2 * [l(x,y)] * [w(x,y)] \quad (5.3)$$

Step7: Repeat steps 2 to 5 until the meaningful gesture is identified.

5.3.2. Subunit Modelling

Subunit modelling involves training and modelling the signs with extracted features in the form of subunits. Signs are composed of both manual and non-manual features. Representation of single sign using single stream HMM is infeasible because one sign is associated with more than one feature. Similarly, each sign has to be represented by the simultaneous aspects of both hands and face, so it is not possible with single HMM to handle the parallel aspects of sign language. The formation of the subunit from each vector is depicted in figure 5.2.

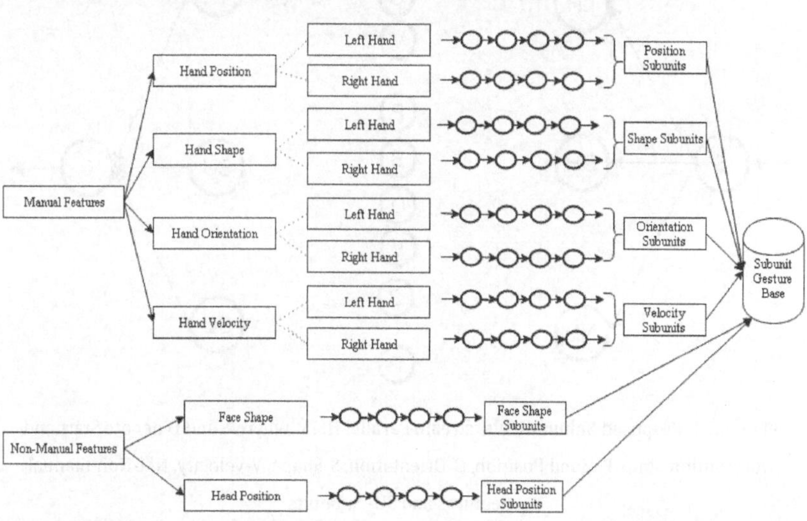

Figure 5.2: Modelling of Subunits from Manual and Non-Manual Features

The proposed system generates subunits based on the following steps. At first, the continuous video sequence that consists of continuous sign sentences is considered. In the next step, these video sentences are segmented in the range of 30 frames per second to make it as a set of isolated signs. Then for each sign based on chapter 3 the features are extracted and they are treated as subunits, and the provided advantages of proposed subunit modelling are that when two different signs have two or more similar features, then these features will be clustered in one class to reduce the gesture base space and to provide the inter-gloss vocabulary access. Finally, all these feature distributions are shared on their own channel in multi-stream PaHMM to form the subunits. The Subunit Multi-stream Parallel HMM model is illustrated in figure 5.3. The likelihood of each stream in PaHMM is calculated using the following equation.

$$P(O|\lambda_{manual}).P(O|\lambda_{non-manual}) = \pi_{\lambda=1}^{s} P(O_{smanual}|\lambda_{smanual}) + P(O_{snon-manual}|\lambda_{snon-manual}), \sum_{s}^{S} W_s = 1 \quad (5.4)$$

where $P(O_{smanual} | \lambda_{smanual})$ and $P(O_{snon-manual} | \lambda_{snon-manual})$ is the likelihood of the manual and non-manual features in the stream S respectively. And Ws represents the weight between the streams.

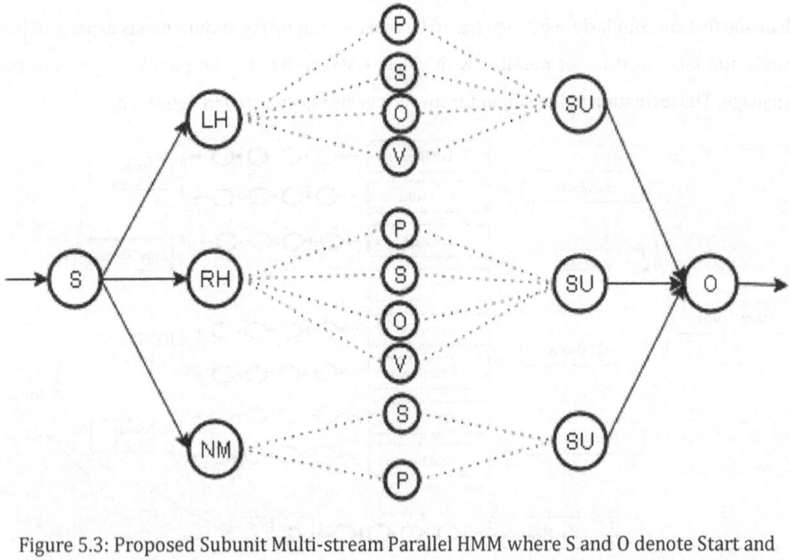

Figure 5.3: Proposed Subunit Multi-stream Parallel HMM where S and O denote Start and Observation State, P-Hand Position, O-Orientation, S-Shape, V-velocity, NM-Non-manual Features and SU- Subunits

5.3.3. Epentheses Movement Identification

Epentheses movements are modelled and dynamically clustered and pruned in this proposed approach. Unlike other approaches, it is neither modelled explicitly nor left without modelling these movements. Since epentheses movement modelling is generally a time- consuming process and needs more human groundwork for manual labelling; it affects the system scalability. The proposed research work preferred not to model such movements in the trained gesture base. At the same time, when it is left unmodelled these movements affects the system performance by making numerous comparisons with the gesture base.

The proposed system aims in focusing on extracting the subunits and modeling these subunits to form the trained gesture base. Epentheses movements are those that are not signs but only the hand transitions between the signs. These movements are not present in the constructed gesture base. While classifying the sign gestures, the considerable transition movements will be clustered during exploitation instead of training. Therefore, the gesture base deals only with the base of lexicons of subunits signs and not with epentheses movements, so the gesture base will not occupy more space. Figure 5.4 depicts the dynamic epentheses movement modelling.

The process of dynamic pruning of epentheses movements is presented to segment the hand transition between the signs. This dynamic iteration process is explained in the following steps:

1. Extracted features and framed subunits for the recorded text sentence videos along with sign lexicons are stored in the gesture base.
2. Segment the video sequence as 30 frames per second and set the transition state as the last frame of the ending sign and the first frame of the preceding sign.
3. Using SMP-HMM, the simultaneous aspects of two hands and face were recognized, the proposed work used one channel of HMM for recognizing one feature.
4. Dynamically cluster the epentheses movements using spatiotemporal clustering. Then compare the remaining segmented sign portion with the gesture base to classify the appropriate signs and save all these as isolated signs.
5. Repeat steps 2 and 3 until all the epentheses movements are clustered for a sentence. Otherwise, classify the signs with the trained gestures.

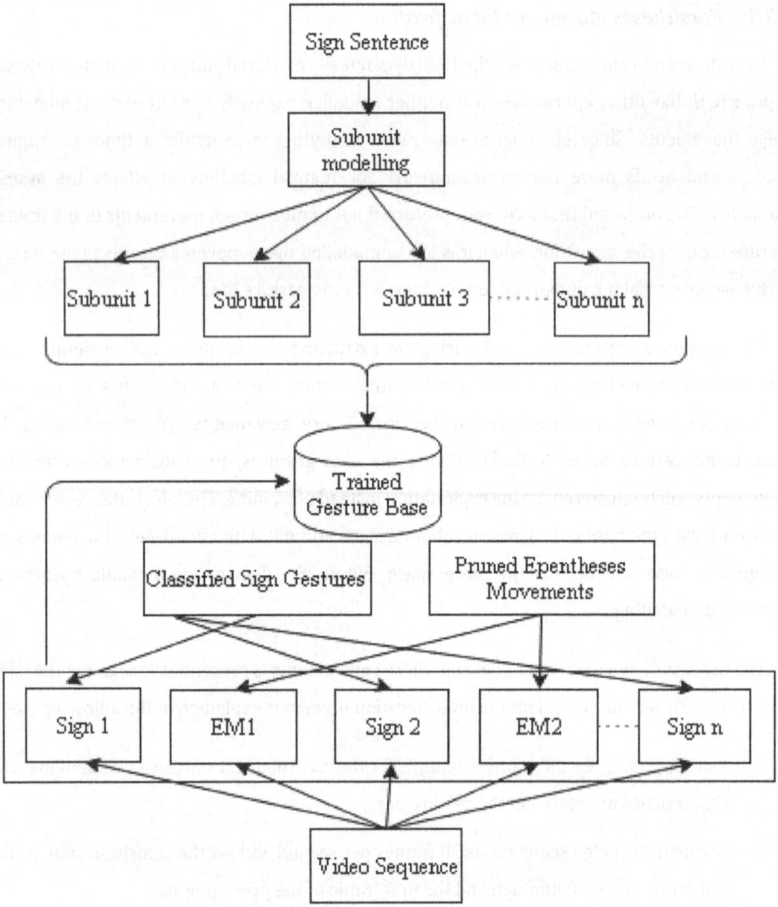

Figure 5.4: Subunit Modelling for Epentheses Movements

Epentheses movements are dynamically constructed to improve the system performance. On the other hand, the computation cost needs to be saved while considering large vocabulary signs. The most important parts that need to be considered before eliminating epentheses movements are the active part of the signs. In a current frame, only a small probability of the sign is present. This means that the frame need not be examined further. Due to the continuous trajectory property of signs, it indirectly illustrates that the active portions are present in the previous frames. The proposed work adheres to the following steps to prune the collected epentheses movements.

1. Except the last frame, calculate the probability of the first state for rest of the frames. When the probability of the frame is high, then that word is chosen as candidate word for the current set of frames. Classify that gesture as a selected sign for the active portion based on computation and the rest of the frames are not considered as examining frames.
2. For the last frames, compute the threshold probability. When the probability is lower than the threshold, then such frames are treated as epentheses movements and pruned dynamically during classification.

5.3.4. *EDP Iteration*

The proposed EDP iteration model handles both spatial and temporal feature vectors to cluster and remove epentheses movements dynamically. Epentheses movements do not have any reasonable measure to accumulate the number of clusters. Based on the spatial information, it is infeasible to cluster the hand transition since it is based on time-series vectors. Therefore, the proposed approach is expected to be developed and implemented on the basis of epentheses movement distribution in all over the frames. Li et al. 2004 introduced Minimum Entropy clustering algorithm and proved that it out performs significantly than the other clustering algorithms namely K-means, hierarchical, SOM and EM algorithms. Therefore, Minimum Entropy Clustering is adapted to cluster the spatial features and enhanced using dynamic programming approach to cluster the temporal feature vectors.

In this research work, dynamic time warping is incorporated with MEC for clustering epentheses movements. Based on this clustering, distance between temporal vectors of the hand trajectories is calculated along with the spatial features of hands. This calculation is done on the basis of recursive iterations, until all the epentheses movements have been collected between the adjacent signs. To minimize the distance between two sequence frames of temporal feature vectors, this dynamic programming is used:

Let p and q be the two temporal sequences. The time warping function is calculated as

$$d(p,q) = \min_{\theta} \sum_{n=1}^{N} d(\theta p(n), \theta q(n)) \tag{5.5}$$

where d(p,q) is the search to compute the minimal distance between the temporal sequence and warping path of the frames. P is the first temporal sequence {p(1),p(2),....p(n)}, q is the second temporal sequence {q(1),q(2),....q(n)}, ɵ is the time warping function {ɵ(1), ɵ(2),.....

ɵ(n)}=(ɵ(p(n)), ɵ(q(n))), Nis the normal duration of occurrence of two temporal sequences and n is the matching pair that consists of the ɵ(p(n)) feature in p and ɵ(q(n)) feature in q.

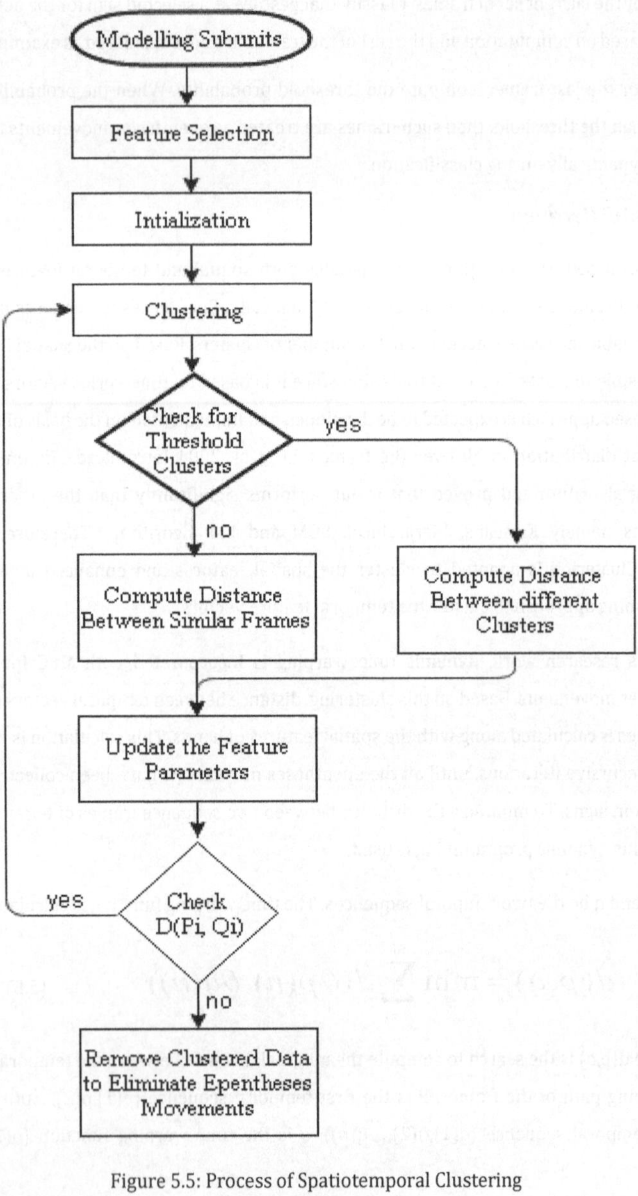

Figure 5.5: Process of Spatiotemporal Clustering

The recursive iteration of such distance and warping path computation is done by following the equation given below.

$$D(P_i,Q_i)=\arg\min_{(iP,iQ)}[d(i_P',i_Q')+d(i_P+i_Q)] \tag{5.6}$$

where (i_p',i_q') is the dynamic programming warping path to obtain the minimum distance sequence to efficiently obtain in different iterations. The obtained D(P_i, Q_i) is used while clustering the frames to eliminate epentheses movements and to accurately classify the sign features. The process flow of spatiotemporal clustering is shown in figure 5.5.

This proposed system is implemented based on the Parallel Hidden Markov Model for feature selection and extraction. The initial segmentation is done on the feature level. For a particular sign, a set of observation sequences are collected and they are initialized as the expected number of cluster C_n for n iterations. C_k is the distance between consecutive frames to determine which frames need to be clustered either consecutive frames or random frames in the first iteration.

After computing the minimum distance, D(P_i, Q_i), the sample is classified to find the corresponding cluster center. If the clusters are less than the collected samples, then the cluster is discarded as epentheses movements. Otherwise the clusters need to be checked to find the corresponding sign from the gesture base. Once the clusters are found, check for the iterations nmod2=0 and expected number of cluster to form the cluster center Cn>c to form the consecutive or random frames between the sign frames. Consecutive clusters are formed based on two temporal sequences on condition that they satisfy d(cp1, cp2) < Cn, then combine p1 and q1. Let the warping function be Θ and the cluster formed as

$$C_k=\frac{1}{2}(C(p)\theta_k+C(q)\theta_k),k=1,2,3,\ldots n \tag{5.7}$$

5.4. Results and Discussions

5.4.1. Data Sets

There are three different data sets used to test the system performance of the proposed system and it is listed in table 5.1. The data is chosen based on three criteria. The first gesture base set GB1 chosen for the experiment consisting of a long sleeve and a simple background. The second data set GB2 comprising self-captured videos with complex, cluttered background, textured and short sleeves. The third data set chosen here comprised of continuous sentence text corpus where the background is complex but static.

Table 5.1: Summary of datasets

Parameters	GB1	GB2	GB3
Background	Simple, Static	Complex, textured	Complex, static
Sleeves of signers	Long	Short	Not used
Number of signers	3	3	3
Resolution of training and testing videos	320X240	640X480	640X290
Training videos	50	100	100
Testing videos	50(randomly chosen)	50(20 randomly chosen and 30 new videos)	50(20 randomly chosen, 10 new videos and 20 from third signer)
Testing videos present in training	Yes	Yes, but 30 new videos were used for testing	Yes, but 10 new videos and 20 videos from new signer were used for testing
Single/double handed signs	Both	Both	Both
Isolated/ Continuous signs	Both	Both	Both
Epenthesis Movements	Not present	Present	Present
Manual/Non-Manual Signs	Manual	Both	Both

Experimental data consists of 100 distinct video sequences for isolated signs and 350 continuous video sequences from three different signers, where two signers were used to train the system and one signer was used to test the system. Two experiments were conducted to prove the system efficiency across signer independence validation and variations. The results obtained were also tested under different illuminations, orientations and distances. The first experiment was conducted to identify the efficiency of epentheses movement identification and pruning in the continuous sign sentences and the other experiment was conducted to test the performance of the proposed EDP approach among other approaches used in sign recognition. These results are discussed in detail for getting a clear substantiation towards sign language recognition.

Experiment 1: Epentheses Movement Identification

As the proposed system has its direct influence on the direct recognition of continuous sign sentence, it has to prove at first, that the isolated signs could be identified from the continuous sequence. All the features used to recognize the sign sentences are based on parallel HMM where one channel represents one feature and the discriminative feature selection is used to choose the best feature identification based on the area-under-the-curve measure. These channels collect only the subunits of both manual and non-manual signs and then classify the sign gesture without using explicit modelling of epentheses movements.

From the three data sets, 75 samples from each data set were chosen randomly, totally 225 samples were used to test the framework performance in identifying the epentheses movements. All these data sets are coloured and are in the range of 30 key frames per second. The accuracy of epenthesis movement identification is calculated based on three error parameters namely insertion (I), deletion (D) and substitution(S). It is estimated as

$$Accuracy = \frac{No.\ of\ correctly\ \text{clustered epentheses movements}\ (C)}{\text{Total No.}\ of\ \text{sign gestures used for testing}\ (N)} \tag{5.8}$$

The accuracy is evaluated based on the ratio of the number of correctly clustered epentheses movements C and it is calculated as N- (S + D) to the total number of sign gestures used for testing. The epentheses movement identification is done using two signers for training and one signer for testing the proof-of-cross sign validation. The data set GB1 is analyzed for signer independence and transition movement classification; it shows that the proposed EDP framework produces an accuracy percentage of 100 in identifying the cross signer sign gestures. Since it is an isolated gesture, the evaluation is done only for signer independence.

Table 5.2: Accuracy of Epentheses Movement Identification

Data Sets	N	C	Errors			Accuracy (%)	Recognition/ Computation time (s/w)
			S	I	D		
GB1	75	75	0	0	0	100	0.57
GB2	75	73	3	1	1	97.4	0.62
GB3	75	74	2	2	0	98.6	0.59
Average						**98.6**	**0.59**

Table 5.2 shows the results achieved for all three data sets which are different data sets in the aspect of recognizing epentheses movements. The recognition rate shows an average of 0.59 seconds to recognize such movements from the continuous video sequence. This result also

validates the cross-signer verification in performing sign gesture in GB3 and provides an accuracy of 98.6% in complex backgrounds. From the above results, it is proved that the proposed system out performs with an average of 97.4% in highly cluttered environment and 98.6% in static background. This shows the variation of only 1.2% in different backgrounds and illuminations.

The total error rate while identifying epentheses movements are marked in figure 5.6. The rate of recognition is evaluated for three different data sets GB1, GB2 and GB3. The test results are reported by equally increasing the number of testing sequences in the range of 20 samples per data set. From the graph, the proposed system illustrates that it has the average error rate of 4 to 6% even though the number of testing samples were increased. For an average increase of 20 samples in testing sequence, the proposed EDP framework shows a variation of 1% error rate. After thorough observation, it is concluded that the proposed work has the efficiency to yield better accuracy and less error rate for large vocabulary sign gestures.

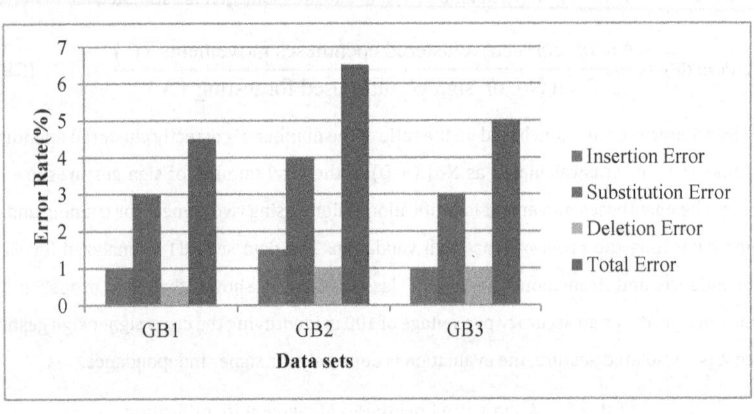

Figure 5.6: Total Sign Level Error Rate in Recognizing Epentheses Movements using EDP Framework

Experiment 2: Comparison with Existing Models

The aim of this experiment was to evaluate the performance of the proposed EDP framework with other models. As the proposed work is developed without any explicit modelling of epentheses movements, the result of the proposed model is compared with the performance of Hidden Markov Model, context dependent models and conditional random fields. Table 5.3 exhibits the comparison of other approaches in a continuous sign sequence in SLR. All three data sets were tested with existing approaches which includes HMM, Threshold HMM (THMM), Gesture Threshold HMM (GTHMM), Conditional Random Fields (CRF) and Latent Dynamic

Conditional Random Fields (LDCRF). To evaluate the recognition result of these approaches with proposed EDP framework, about 450 different sentences were used to test the framework performance in all three different data sets GB1, GB2 and GB3.

The proposed EDP framework outperforms when compared with other HMM and CRF models. This EDP approach follows the technique of Parallel HMM but the novelty lies in feature selection. The feature selection for proposed work is based on the subunits of signs and for fair comparison with other existing works; the proposed EDP approach is named in results as Subunit Multi-stream Parallel HMM. These results were recorded for large vocabulary signs by extending the number of signs in all three data sets. Experimental results have proved that the SMP-HMM shows tremendous improvement in recognition rate and performance when compared models with explicitly or implicitly trained movement epentheses and without movement epentheses.

Table 5.3: Comparison of Proposed SMP-HMM with Different Existing Models in SLR

Model	GB1	GB2	GB3	Average Accuracy (%)
HMM	0.930	0.910	0.925	92.2
THMM	0.943	0.919	0.932	93.1
GT-HMM	0.977	0.976	0.977	97.7
SMP-HMM (Proposed Approach)	0.995	0.985	0.986	98.9
CRF	0.870	0.830	0.846	84.9
LDCRF	0.920	0.890	0.915	90.8

From table 5.3, it is inferred that the SMP-HMM shows a recognition accuracy of 98.9% on the test set of over 450 different sentences which then increases in its accuracy of 7.7%, 4.8% and 1.2 % when compared with HMM, THMM and GT-HMM models respectively. Similarly when compared with other context dependent models, the proposed system shows an average accuracy improvement of over 14% in CRF and 8.1% in LDCRF. Therefore, the experiments have proved that the system with explicit or implicit modelling of epentheses movements is able to handle only a small set of vocabulary signs. At the same time, systems without modelled or trained epentheses movements to handle large vocabulary signs but unfortunately accuracy of those systems is quite less when compared with the accuracy of explicit modelling. The proposed approach, on the other hand, has ability to solve both these issues and produce an accuracy percentage of over 98% for large vocabulary signs.

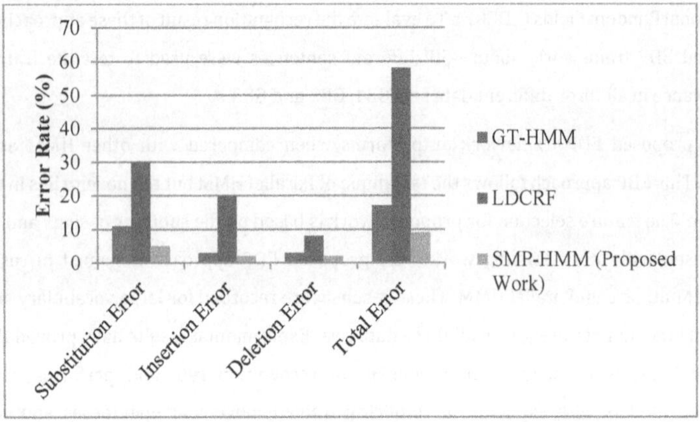

Figure 5.7: Comparison of Error Rate for Movement Epentheses Classification Models

GT-HMM, dedicated gesture models and LDCRF, context dependent models, are the closest one in performance with the EDP approach in identifying and classifying the epentheses movements. Therefore, the error rate of the SMP-HMM was evaluated and compared only with these two models and the results are plotted in figure 5.7. The test was conducted for all three gesture base with 150 samples each performing multimodal sign gestures by different signers. The results obtained have shown that the SMP-HMM produces more accuracy in recognition and a less error rate when compared with the other two models. The error rate for SMP-HMM is reduced from 17 to 9% when compared with GT-HMM, and when compared with LDCRF, there is tremendous decrease in the error rate from 58 to 9% where 49% of error rates are reduced using the proposed approach.

5.5. Summary

This proposed research work designed, developed and explored an EDP framework to classify spatiotemporal sign gestures and epentheses movements in continuous sign sentences in SLR. To address these unsolved major issues in continuous SLR, SMP-HMM is based on spatiotemporal clustering and dynamic time warping techniques. The proposed approach does not require any explicit modelling for identifying epentheses movements. Hence the scalability of the system remains constant and the computation cost is also very less. The gestures are the ones that are involved in training for continuous sign sentence and isolated signs but not the epentheses movements in the proposed framework. Current systems find it difficult to analyze the epentheses movements because when the vocabulary grows, the number of epentheses movements would also grow in turn. This would make explicit or implicit modelling of epentheses movements an infeasible process. This research contributes to novel ways of recognizing signs while accounting epentheses movements and also towards the ability to handle hand gesture segmentation ambiguities without any human interventions. Experimental results of proposed EDP framework demonstrate that SMP-HMM has its own relaxation in handling all sorts of restrictions in the background, signer clothing and signer independence. Comparison of performance with other previous explicit models and other HMM models have showed significant improvements in system performance.

CHAPTER VI

6. Subunit Sign Modelling for Sign Language Recognition from Continuous Sign Sequences

6.1. Introduction

A novel subunit sign modelling framework is introduced to recognize the large-vocabulary multi-modal signs from continuous video sequences constituting different sign languages. The proposed approach involves spatial and temporal modelling of subunits using the BPaHMM and constructs the spatio-temporal sequentiality of subunits without any prior linguistic information in an unsupervised behaviour. The sequentiality of spatial and temporal subunits are constructed based on feature extraction and feature selection discussed in chapter 3, the proposed subunit modelling constructs the sign lexicon for one spatial subunit (hand shape) and two temporal subunits (velocity and position). Hence the constructed sign lexicon is named as (three subunits) and the proposed approach is called as Subunit Sign Modelling Framework.

A Bayesian Network is employed to handle the classification of spatial and temporal subunits. After that, an HMM model is adopted to recombine these subunits where the first state corresponds to spatial subunits and the second state corresponds to temporal subunits. The obtained cues are then clustered based on the behaviour as spatial and temporal subunits using Minimum Entropy Clustering and Dynamic Time Warping techniques and formed the sign lexicon based on data-driven approach. After obtaining the subunits based on the constructed sign lexicon and its corresponding cluster, each subunit is trained using Subunit Multi-stream Parallel HMM based on Bakis topology. The Viterbi algorithm is adopted to train these PaHMM and find the maximum probability node among all the subunits i.e. the state of the existing subunit from the gesture base. Baum-Welch Algorithm is employed to recalculate the subunit parameters and the recognition begins with the emission probability of each HMM nodes.

6.2. Subunit Sign Modelling Framework

The proposed subunit modelling consists of four components namely Spatial/Temporal (S/T) Subunit Modelling, Construction of S/T Subunits, Sign Lexicon Construction, and Subunit (SU) Training & Recognition. All these four components play a significant role in subunit modelling to achieve a better performance in SLR. The first major contribution of this proposed research work is Spatial/Temporal (S/T) Subunit Modelling. One of the most essential features of sign language is velocity cues. With the help of this velocity feature, recognition of signs even in very critical situations can also be achieved with ease. The next contribution of this research is the construction of S/T Subunits. This is achieved by extracting all the cues namely hand shape, convexity hull, convexity defects and hand trajectory information. The first three cues are spatial where as the trajectories which consist of position, orientation and velocity are the temporal features. Finally the three SU-level sign lexicon for hand shape, velocity and position is constructed based on feature selection strategies. These three cues play a vital role in yielding better recognition rate of signs.

Another part of the contribution is constructing sign lexicon in SU level. is constructed for hand shape, velocity and position. Once the spatial and temporal subunits (hand shape subunit along with position and velocity subunits) are obtained in an unsupervised manner, all the cues are combined to form the corresponding sign lexica without any manual interventions. Final contribution of this framework is Training & Recognition of obtained SUs. The proposed work employs SMP-HMM to integrate and to train the hand shape (HS), position (P) and velocity (V) cues. The trained SU models and lexicons are obtained separately for HS, P and V. In recognition, the proposed system finds both S/T SUs by identifying the most probable SU per segment among other S/T SUs. This results in obtaining the sequence of S/T SUs to recognize the continuous signs. The proposed SU Sign Modelling Framework is shown in figure 6.1.

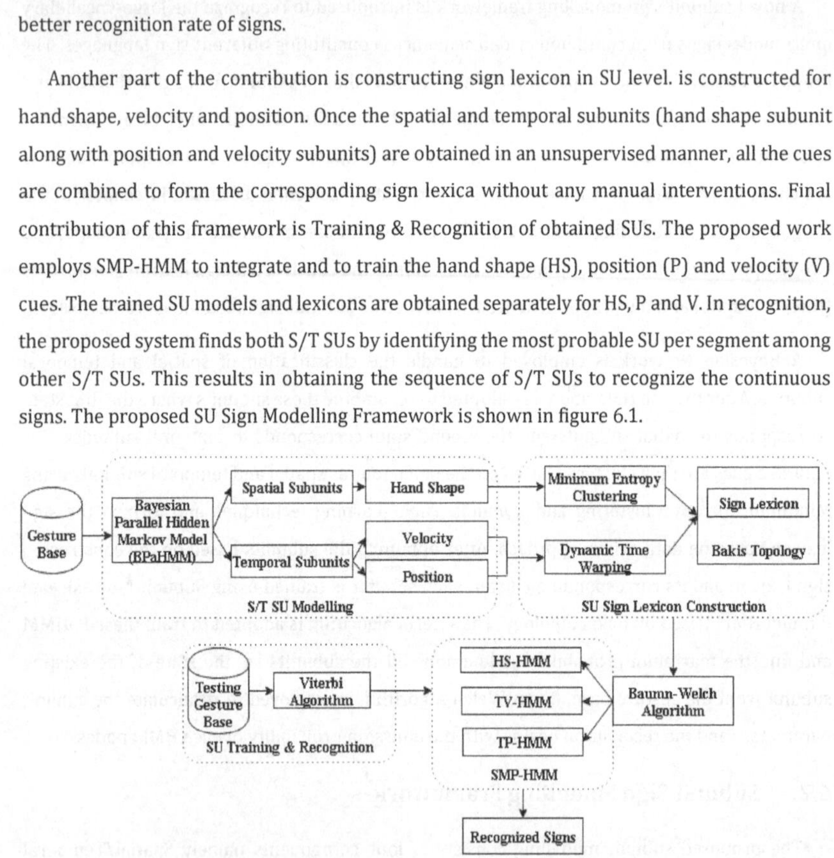

Figure 6.1: Proposed Framework and its Components for Automatic Sign Language Recognition

6.2.1. S/T Subunit Modelling

The major concern in SU sign modelling is segmenting signs into sub-sign segments and classifying such segments as S/T SUs. This classification is purely based on hand movements and postures. The spatial SUs are considered as static postures which do not involve in any transitions whereas the temporal subunits are those with transitions. The spatial subunits are constructed from hand shape and the temporal subunits are constructed from position and velocity of hands during transitions. A Bayesian Network is employed to handle the classification of spatial and temporal subunits. After that, a HMM model is adapted to recombine these subunits where the first state corresponds to spatial subunits and the second state corresponds to temporal subunits.

After obtaining the subunits, the next step is to train those subunits. The Viterbi algorithm is adapted to train these PaHMM and find the maximum probability node among all the subunits i.e. state of the existing subunit from the gesture base. Baum-Welch Algorithm is employed to recalculate the feature parameters. Figure 6.2 shows the structure of BPaHMM in classifying the S/T SUs. In this figure, S represents Sign gestures i.e. observation of input sequences, hSt represents hidden state of Spatial cues with respect to observation time t and hS_t represents hidden state of Temporal cues with respect to observation time t and $S/T^{1...n}$ represents Spatial/Temporal SUs output sequence after segmentation.

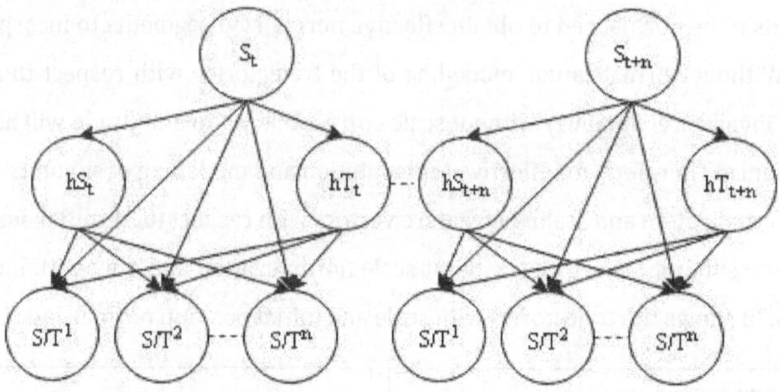

Figure 6.2: Illustration of BPaHMM for S/T SU Segmentation

6.2.2. Construction of S/T Subunits

S/T SUs are clustered after the segmentation and modelled with Multi-stream Parallel HMM. Spatial Subunits are constructed based on extracted hand shape using the Fourier descriptors. Once all the SUs are obtained, all the frames are considered to cluster with MEC where each clusters corresponding to different SUs. As a result, similar hand shapes of different signs are clustered accordingly. This allows the gesture base to be shared by two or more similar SUs. Temporal subunits are constructed by considering the transition movements. Based on the velocity of transition, the subunit is considered as hand velocity or hand position. By calculating the average frequency of frames i.e. 30 key frames per second, the frame with high transition movement is treated as velocity cue where as the frames with less transition movements are treated as position SUs.

The hand position information is obtained from the trajectories based on the Euclidean distance. The occurrence of the first position of the hand is computed based on the starting point of the hand in the first frame and the centroid of the hand trajectories. Similarly, the occurrence of the second position of hand coordinates are calculated based on the distance between the starting point and the current point of the hand coordinates in consecutive frames. Once hand shape, hand position and hand velocity SUs are obtained, all these SUs are clustered. Since position and velocity are based on temporal information, Minimum Entropy Clustering alone is not enough to cluster the temporal SUs. It is required to incorporate the temporal data by using Dynamic Time Warping technique. Finally, all these distances are clustered to get the end criterion for number of clusters for temporal SUs. Due to temporal clustering, each SU in gesture base refers to both velocity and position cues where as hand shape cue will be concatenated during training as separate SU.

Before clustering, the direction or the scale of the feature vectors with respect to the initial position needs to be normalized to obtain effective normalized segments to incorporate model invariance. Without normalization, modelling of the trajectories with respect to position will increase the invariance. Similarly without scale corresponding to amplitude will also affect the model invariance. Therefore, for effective segmentation and modelling of subunits, modelling is done with normalization and scaling of feature vectors with respect to its initial position. Figure 6.3a shows the subunit trajectories without scale normalization and only with initial position and Figure 6.3b shows the trajectories with scale and initial position normalization.

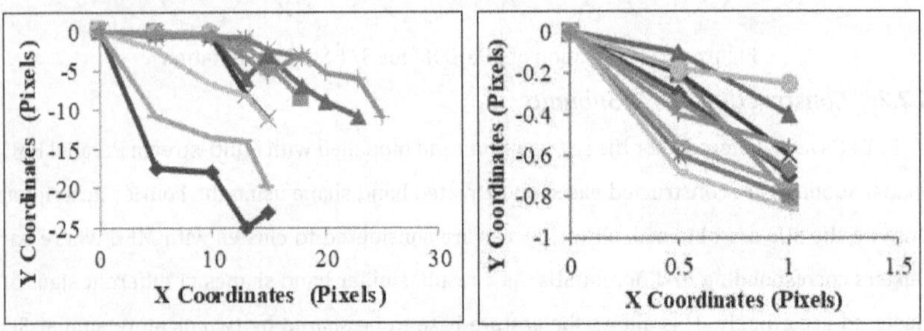

(a) (b)

Figure 6.3: Mapping of Trajectories into 2D Signing Space. a) After Initial Position Normalization and b) After Initial Position and Scale Normalization

6.2.3. *Sign Lexicon Construction*

Sign Lexicon is constructed without any prior knowledge on phonetic transcriptions, annotations or manual labelling. Data-Driven approach is followed to construct the sign lexicon by combining hand shape, and position and velocity features. These are obtained from S/T SU construction and then the constructed lexicon is used for SU training and recognition. After segmenting and clustering S/T SUs, they is united together to get the lexicon. By this way, the sign lexicon consists of an entry in the gesture base for each SU. Every SU in the gesture base consists of Spatial (S) or Temporal (T) SU label along with the assigned cluster id.

For spatial SUs, the label is assigned as S along with the cluster id and for the temporal SUs; the label is assigned as TV for Velocity and TP for position along with the corresponding cluster id. Therefore, the proposed approach constructs lexicon for three subunits and hence this lexicon is named as. is constructed without any explicit or implicit modelling of transition movements and positions. The dominant hand is right hand for processing the lexicon where as the non-dominant hand is considered when both the hands are moving or both the hands are non-moving during transitions. Figure 6.4 explains the example of lexica construction S/T SUs.

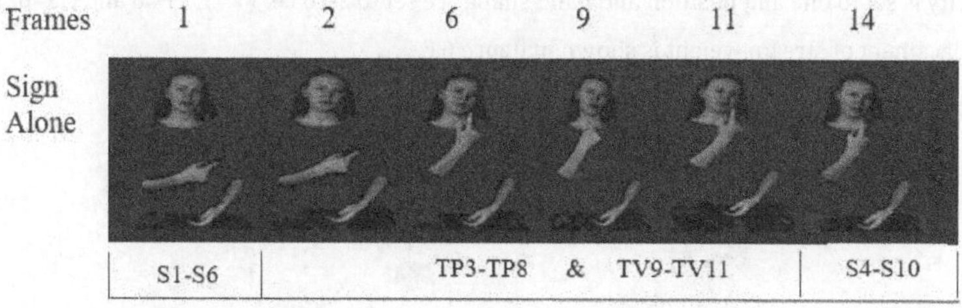

Figure 6.4: Lexicon Constructions for Sign ALONE (ASLLVD)

6.2.4. *SU Training & Recognition*

According to the constructed sign lexicon, each sign is composed of a sequence of S/T SUs. For training and recognition of SU, a SMP-HMM is used. In recognition, the most probable S/T segment needs to be found from the given set of features and from the SU models that best match the S/T segment. The SMP-HMM models the S/T segments by using TV cues, TP cues and S cues for the dominant hand. Similarly, it integrates all the cues for the non-dominant hands. Because HMM alone cannot manage all these cues, Multi-stream HMM is used to train these set of features but the features are segmented based on S/T instances; multi-cue parallelism is used to handle this variations. Hence SMP-HMM is introduced to handle the segments and to train these lexicon. The illustrations are depicted in figure 6.5.

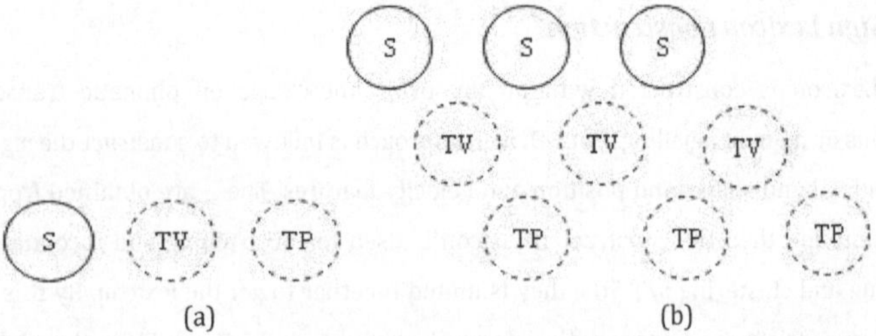

Figure 6.5: SMP-HMM for Multi-cue Parallelism a) S/T Sequence b) S/T Sequence in Multi-Stream

The main concern in implementing the SMP-HMM is setting the stream weight for different cues under different segmentations. Here, the cue segments are considered on the basis of S/T instances. Therefore, each SU has its own stream weight, computed as one for each single stream.

It is assumed in such a way that when the stream follows the spatial SUs, then the movements or velocity instances are set to zero and position cues, set to one. Similarly, hand shapes are set as one i.e. TV=0, TP=1 and HS=1. In the same way when the temporal SUs are considered, velocity is set to one and position and hand shape are set to zero i.e. TV=1, TP=0 and HS=0. This interlacement of stream weight is shown in figure 6.6.

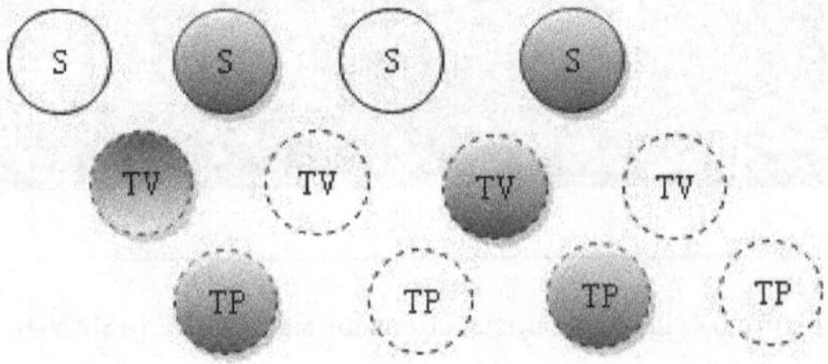

Figure 6.6: Interlacement Across Time in SMP-HMM

These cue segments along with the cluster ids are collected to map the training samples and associated S/T SU models. Based on Bakis topology, SMP-HMM is constructed with two states for T SUs and one state for S SUs. The Viterbi algorithm is engaged to train these HMM and to find the majority plausible state sequence in a repetitive manner. Once training is completed, parameters of HMM is estimated i.e. logging likelihood of all the training data. This process is repeated until all the data are trained without further increase in likelihood of the HMM parameters.

After this training, Baum-Welch algorithm is applied to re-calculate the parameter values for both spatial and temporal SUs. When all the training samples are processed, the total accumulative set of statistical values of HMM and temporal HMM is re-estimated. When the training is complete, sign instances need to be recognized based on the constructed subunit models. The subunit recognition is done based on the trained HMM along with the constructed SU lexicon. In this way, the recognition begins with each node in the HMM emitting a state through the exact path for a test example t with T frames. All the path values have to be calculated and summed to find the individual transition log-probability and also the log-probability of emitting node. The most probable S/T sequence at each time instance is computed to maximize the above log-probability estimated from each path in the recognition network.

6.3. Experimental Results

6.3.1. Phonetic SU Construction and Construction

The Phonetics-Based SU (Pitsikalis et al. 2011) can only be used when the phonetic transcriptions are available for all the signs but these kind of low-level annotations are time-consuming. For an alternative strategy, the implementation has to work either towards phonetic adaptation or to proceed with new models to account for missing phonetic labels. And also, the usual issue arises when training the unequal feature space because with phonetic labels, the gesture base will be highly populated. The main characteristic of the proposed approach is unsupervised recognition of Static (S) corresponds to non-movements and Temporal (T) corresponds to movement SUs. In this way, the final SU model consists of information on trajectories that divides the spatial information and at the same time it incorporates the data-driven information for the efficient recognition of Static (Hand Shape) and Temporal (Velocity and Position) SUs.

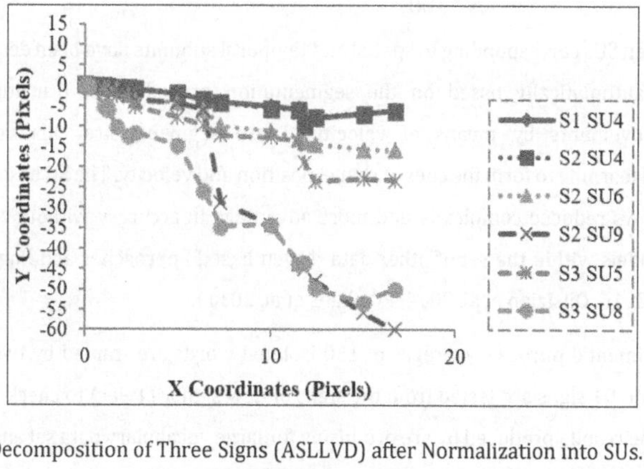

Figure 6.7: Decomposition of Three Signs (ASLLVD) after Normalization into SUs. S1 "Any", S2 "Abroad" and S3 "Child"

To be specific, the proposed approach decodes each feature sequence using Viterbi algorithm in HMM space, and generates the sequential SU labels with the starting and ending frames of all the signs. With the help of this mechanism, the intra-sign SUs are concatenated as lexicons in the gesture base based on the boundaries of S/T SUs for all the sign sequences. Each subunit in the lexicon consists of transition-based information along with the position and hand shape information for all the signs in the vocabulary of ASLLVD data set. The decomposition of signs into subunits for three different signs ANY, ABROAD and CHILD from ASLLVD data set after normalization with respect to initial position and scale is shown in figure 6.7.

The experiments are conducted on data set of ASLLVD for ASL word recognition which consists of almost 3300 different signs and 9800 distinct sign video instances of six native ASL signers. Each sign consists of an average of at least five utterances. To evaluate the performance of signed sentences, the RWTH-PHOENIX-Weather data set is used which consists of 5356 sentences of 1081 distinct signs performed by 7 different signers. To evaluate the accuracy of sign detection for large vocabulary, two metrics are employed: sign accuracy and sign correct. Sign correctness is measured as total number of signs (N) subtracted by the sign Deletion (D) and Substitution (S) i.e. (N-D-S) divided by the total number of signs and multiplied by 100. Sign accuracy is calculated as total number of signs (N) subtracted from the sign Deletion (D), Substitution (S) and Insertion (I) divided by the total number of signs and multiplied by 100.

$$Correctness = \frac{(N-D-S)}{N*100} \tag{5.1}$$

$$Accuracy = \frac{(N-D-S-I)}{N*100} \tag{5.2}$$

Data-Driven SUs corresponding to spatial and temporal subunits have been decomposed and constructed automatically based on the segmentation procedure of transition and non-transition movements by means of velocity. These segments are clustered based on unsupervised learning to form the cues of shape, position and velocity. The SU based data-driven approach shows reduced complexity and more advantage in accuracy without combining the phonetics models within the set of other data-driven based approaches and linguistic models (Koller et al. 2016, Dilsizian et al. 2014, Pitsikalis et al. 2011).

For experimental purpose, averages of 150 isolated words are trained by two signers (Liz and Brady) and 91 signs are tested from the signs of new signer (Tyler) to check for cross-sign validation. The results produced by are promising for large vocabulary data set and it shows the improvement of 32.3% with the reduced error rate of 2% for isolated signs.

To evaluate the accuracy of signed sentences, RWTH-PHOENIX-Weather data set is used where two signers are used for training and one signer is used for testing the signed sentences. From the corpus, 150 sentences are used in total along with tested sentences. The proposed approach shows the reduced error rate of 16.4% from 33.4% when compared with Koller et al. (2016) and produces an average accuracy of 88.7% in signed sentences without using any linguistic modelling. Experimental results are depicted in figure 6.8 and figure 6.9 to prove the sign classification accuracy of proposed.

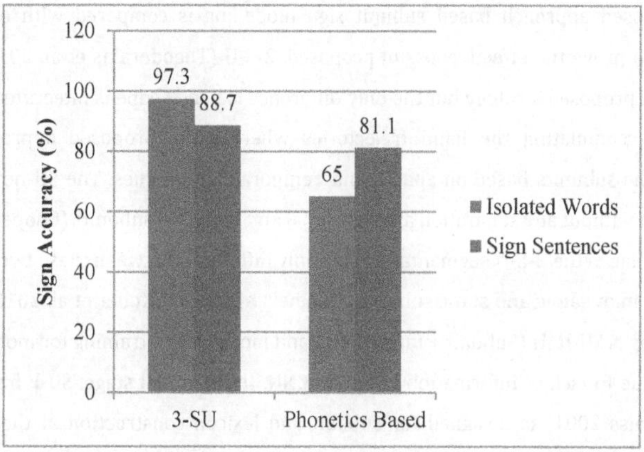

Figure 6.8: Comparison of Data-Driven based Approaches and Linguistics based Approaches

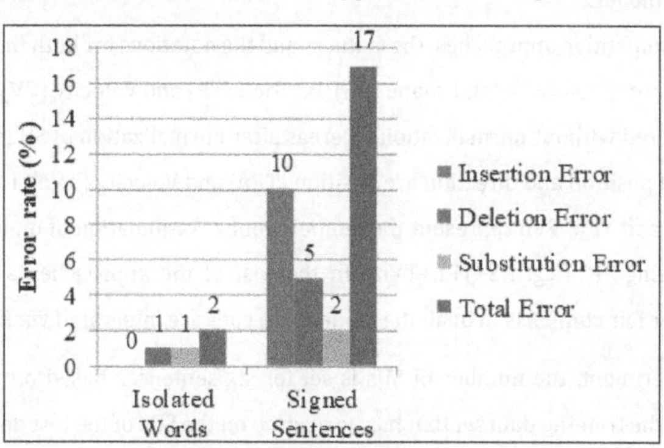

Figure 6.9: Total Number of Error in Isolated Words and Continuous Signs

6.3.2. Experiments on RWTH-PHOENIX-Weather Data Set

Recognition experiments on RWTH-PHOENIX-Weather data set are engaged to test the accuracy of proposed approach by taking into the account of transitions of both the hands and shape of the dominant hand (right hand). The evaluation criterion is set as follows: Signer

Dependent Experiments that is training and testing with same signer on large corpus of data. Cross-Signer Validation is done based on training with signer A and testing with signer B. RWTH-PHOENIX-Weather data employed in the recognition experiments consists of an vocabulary of 1200 signs and almost 5356 sentences of about 600k frames signed by seven different signers but the data are not equally partitioned. All recorded videos are at 25 frames per second and the size of the frames is 210 X 260 pixels. Based on experimental results, the video frame size is reduced and cropped to 50 X 70 pixels because the hands are exactly cropped within this range.

The proposed approach based subunit sign modelling is compared with other similar approaches to prove the effectiveness of proposed. 2-S-U (Theodorakis et al. 2014) is almost similar to the proposed strategy but the only difference is hand shape is integrated in the later stage after accumulating the hand trajectories whereas the proposed approach initially categorizes the subunits based on Spatial and Temporal feature cues. The SU-noST approach segmentation without any separation among spatial and temporal subunits (Cooper et al. 2012) is almost similar to the 2-S-U segmentation; the only difference between these two approaches is separation in dynamic and static subunits. The next approach (Koller et al. 2015) in subunit sign modelling is SU-IMH (Subunit + image net -hand motion). Pre-training for motion of hands is required due to lack of information model in CNN. In the initial stage, SU-F frame level SU (Bauer & Kraiss 2001) is designed for subunit and lexicon construction at the frame level without considering the whole segments whereas the rest all four approaches are based on whole-segment models.

For all the competitive approaches, the features and the notations for both the ascendant and auxiliary hands are as follows: Hand shape (HS), Position (TP) and Velocity (TV) are the general features considered without normalization whereas after normalization of SU trajectories with respect to initial position and direction are Position (TPn) and Velocity (TVn). In, HS represents the spatial cues and TPn, TVn represent the temporal ones. Assimilation of multiple features is incorporated using "+" (e.g. HS+TPn+TVn). In the rest of the approaches S/T SUs are not segmented so for fair comparison of all the models, the cues are integrated via PaHMM.

For this experiment, the number of SUs is set for six sentences based on the recognition performance of the training data set that has no overlap on the SUs of the test data set. The used 60, 120 and 300 SUs for TPn, TVn and HS and for the very similar approaches 2-S-U 120, 180 and 660 SUs for position, velocity and hand shape. For the SU-noST, SU-IMH and SU-F, 960,660 and 660 SUs are used for the position, velocity and hand shape cues respectively.

From this setup, it is observed that the SUs used by is very smaller when compared to SU-noST, SU-IMH and SU-F approaches. The similar approach 2-S-U exercised more SUs for hand shape because of late integration of the HS cues when compared with approach. approach employs less number of subunits because of the discrimination between the Spatial and Temporal SUs.

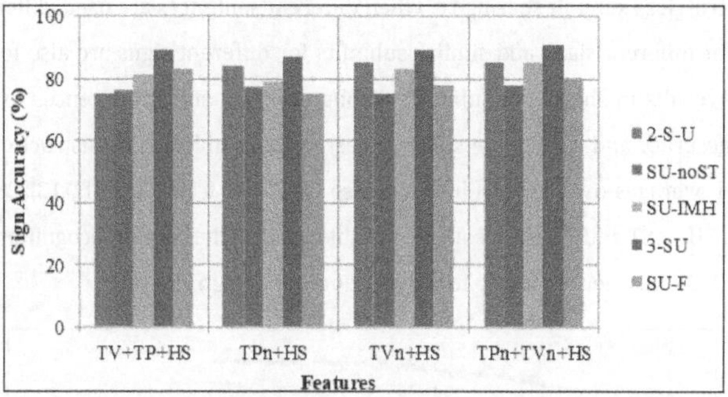

Figure 6.10: Comparison of with Four Existing Subunit Approaches

From the results obtained, it is inferred that outperforms rest of the approaches by employing different features. From figure 6.10, it is noted that the normalized feature vectors produced more accurate results when compared to non-normalized ones and it shows 2% improvement in normalized cues with respect to initial position of scale and direction from non-normalized cues. The proposed shows an average increment of 15.6% and 7.9% when compared with the most similar approach 2-S-U and the more recent approach SU-IMH for the signer dependent classification. This is due to the discrimination between spatial and temporal subunits in the initial stage and the lexicon, constructed based on the three subunits. In the 2-S-U, the hand shape cue is integrated in the latter stage even though there is a discrimination based on static and dynamic cues. This indicates that the feature integration also plays crucial role in recognition and it concerns the integration of different cues as sequential segments not blindly the combination of all cues. Table 6.1 lists the overall recognition accuracy on RWTH-PHOENIX-Weather.

Table 6.1: Overall Recognition Accuracy on RWTH-PHOENIX-Weather between Discriminative Features

Recognition Experiment	Approaches	Subunit Segmentation	S/T Integration	# of Sign Sentences	Sign Accuracy (%)
Features		SMP-HMM	Spatial/ Temporal	Six	91
	2-S-U	2S-Ergodic HMM	Static/ Dynamic		85.3
	SU-noST	2S-Ergodic HMM	NA		78
	SU-IMH	CNN	NA		85
	SU-F	NA	NA		80

Generally while increasing the sign glosses, the recognition performance will be reduced and the error rate will increase. One of the most interesting facts to be noticed from figure 6.11 is improvement in recognition performance when increasing the number of sign sentences. This is due to the intra-gloss subunit sharing i.e. when different sentences are used, different subunits are formed for different signs and similar subunits for different signs are also formed in sign lexicon. This results in sharing of subunits among different signed sentences to increase the recognition accuracy and reduce the space of gesture base in lexicon construction. Therefore, the proposed averages over an absolute increase of 6.78% from SU-IMH, 13.2% from 2-S-U, 20.98% from SU-noST and 23.18% from SU-F. Table 6.2 lists the overall recognition accuracy on RWTH-PHOENIX-Weather according to varying number of sign glosses.

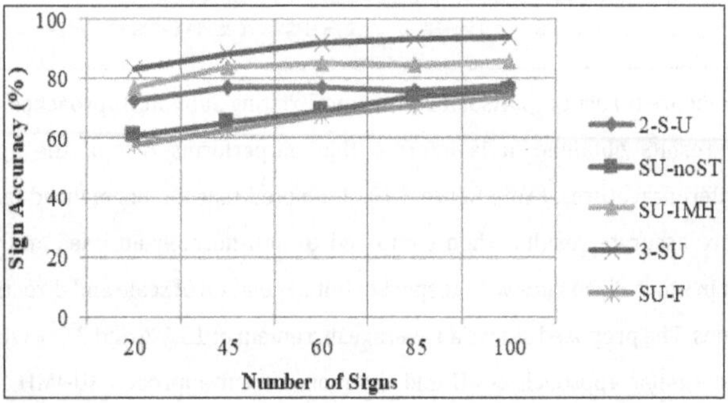

Figure 6.11: Gradual Increments in Number of Signs

The proposed approach is tested for cross-signer validation, that is, no data from the test set is employed in the training data set. Here in the experiment, Signer 1 is performing actions of 304 sentences out of 5356 sentences without any overlap on other signers. Therefore, the proposed is trained with signs of other two signers, Signer 2 and Signer 3, with all repetitions per sign from both the signers and tested efficiency based on unseen signed sentences of Signer 1. From the experimental results obtained, outperforms all the other approaches even in unseen signer conditions with an average accuracy of 88.10%. There is a slight variation of 3% reduction in performance when compared with dependent signers for continuous sign sentences.

When compared with two closest approaches, the SU-IMH and the 2-S-U, shows an improvement of 19.10% and 40% in accuracy for unseen signers respectively. Similarly for cross-signer validation, produces an average accuracy of 91% in multi-signer group sign verification and the corresponding increment in average accuracy is 6% and 6.3% when compared with SU-IMH and 2-S-U whereas it shows 12% and 13% improvement in sign accuracy when compared with SU-F and SU-noST approaches.

Table 6.2: Overall Recognition Accuracy on RWTH-PHOENIX-Weather with Respect to Variation of Signed Sentences

Recognition Experiment	Approaches	Subunit Segmentation	S/T Integration	# of Sign Sentences	Average Accuracy (%)
# Signed Sentences		SMP-HMM	Spatial/ Temporal	{20,45,60, 85,100}	89.98
	2-S-U	2S-Ergodic HMM	Static/ Dynamic		78
	SU-noST	2S-Ergodic HMM	NA		69
	SU-IMH	CNN	NA		83.2
	SU-F	NA	NA		66.8

Also, the proposed approach is tested with the whole-sign based (SW-1) approach (Li et al. 2016) to demonstrate the efficacy of subunit level sign modelling. This whole-sign based approach needs to model the transitions movements along with the signs. This situation leads the system to lose its scalability while considering a large vocabulary sign sentences of RWTH-PHOENIX-Weather dataset.

Also from the acquired results, it is proven that SU level sign modelling outperforms in terms of scalability and accuracy because of its intra-sign SU sharing for large vocabularies and no separate modelling required for transition movements. The proposed produces an improved accuracy of 3.4% for cross-signer validation and 10.10% for unseen signer validation when compared with whole-sign based SLR approach. Experimental results for cross-signer validation and unseen signer verification are listed in table 6.3.

6.3.3. Experiments on ASLLVD Data Set

American Sign Language Lexicon Video Dataset consists of more than 3300 isolated signs from 6 different native ASL signers. For this experiment, the number of SUs is a set based on the recognition performance of the training data set that has no overlap on the SUs of the test data set. The uses 10, 10 and 30 SUs for TPn, TVn and HS for six different signs and for the very similar approaches 2-S-U 20, 30 and 200 SUs for position, velocity and hand shape. For the SU-noST, SU-F and whole-sign based (SW-2) (Dilsizian et al. 2014) 160,200 and 200 SUs are used for the position, velocity and hand shape cues respectively.

Table 6.3: Cross-Signer Validation and Unseen Signer Verification for SU Modelling and Whole-Sign Modelling

Signer	Features		2-S-U	SU-noST	SU-IMH	SU-F	SW-1
Signer 2 & Signer 3	TV+TP+HS	89	75	76	81	83	84.3
	TPn+HS	87	84	77	79	75	85
	TVn+HS	89.3	85	75	83	78	85
	TPn+TVn+HS	91	85.3	78	85	80	87.6
Signer 1	TV+TP+HS	85	30.1	35	58	11.9	72.3
	TPn+HS	85.3	38.8	37.10	61	28.8	75
	TVn+HS	87.4	45.3	38.8	65.3	32.7	75.10
	TPn+TVn+HS	88.10	48	42.6	69	35.53	78

From this setup, it is observed that the SUs used by is very smaller when compared to SU-noST, SU-F and SW-2 based approaches. The similar approach 2-SU exercises more SUs for hand shape because of late integration of the HS cues with static/dynamic cues when compared with approach. approach employs less number of subunits because of the discrimination between the Spatial and Temporal SUs for isolated signs too.

From figure 6.12, it is inferred that the proposed reaches the maximum accuracy of 99.3% in recognizing isolated signs. Comparatively, it produces an improvement of 11.9% from SW-2 where as it shows an increased accuracy even when compared with subunit sign models as well. The proposed produces an increased accuracy of 3.4% from SU-F, 5.2% from 2-S-U and 6.06% from SU-noST approaches.

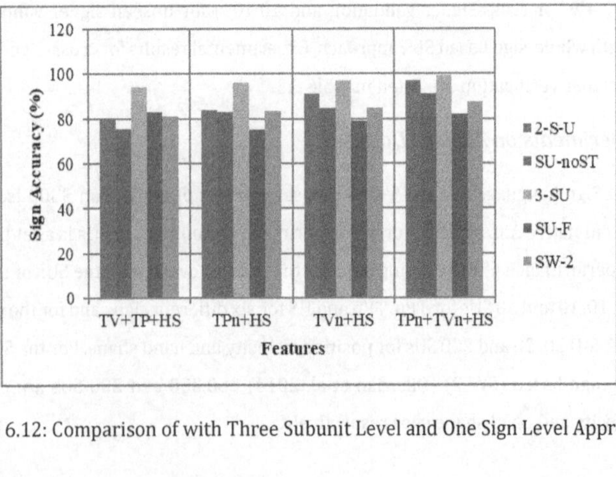

Figure 6.12: Comparison of with Three Subunit Level and One Sign Level Approaches

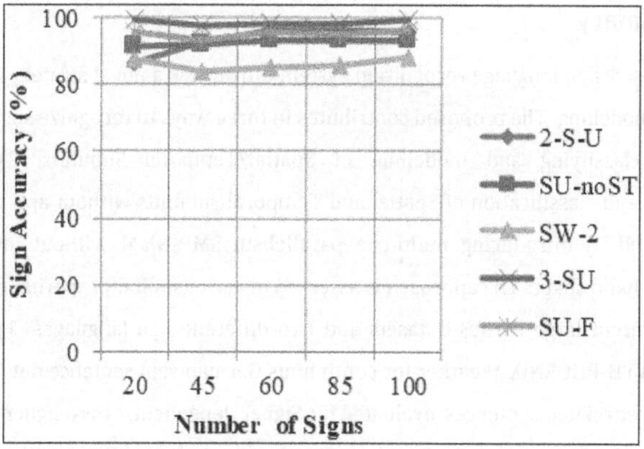

Figure 6.13: Gradual Increments in Number of Signs

Similarly, from figure 6.13, for the varying number of signs from 20 to 100 isolated signs due to intra-gloss subunit sharing the acquires an average efficiency of 98.64%. 2-S-U approach produces an accuracy of 93.4% in average after obtaining the results of 0 to 4 instances but the proposed does not require any instantiation for development data set and produces an improved accuracy in recognition results. Therefore, it is proven that produces effective recognition results when compared with other existing approaches and for large vocabulary data sets. Also, it is proved that the scalability of the system remains constant for increasing vocabulary of signs.

Table 6.4 lists the produced accuracy for unseen signer verification in ASLLVD data set. In this experiment, Signer Lana video sequences were used to train the with one training sample per sign of 3300 signs has been chosen and Signer Dana is tested without any overlap on training sequences. The performance of is tested with all three feature cues in both SU level and SW-2 approaches. It shows relative improvement of 10.9% from 2-S-U, 29.3% from SU-noST, 26.3% from SU-F and 11.9% from SW-2. It is proved that outperforms when compared with other approaches for unseen signer condition with an accuracy of 97.3% for large vocabulary sign lexicons i.e. only 2 percent variation from multi-signer group verification results.

Table 6.4: Accuracy of Unseen Signer Verification in ASLLVD Data Set

Signer	Features		2-S-U	SU-noST	SU-F	SW-2
Signer Lana	TV+TP+HS	95	85.1	65	67	83
	TPn+TVn+HS	97.3	86.4	68	71	85.4

6.4. Summary

The proposed sign language recognition system introduces a novel strategy framework for subunit sign modelling. The proposed contributes in three ways to recognize sign languages. 1) Segmenting, classifying and modelling of Spatial/Temporal Subunits, 2) Data-Driven segmentation and classification of Spatial and Temporal subunits without any prior linguistic knowledge, and 3) introducing multi-cue parallelism SMP-HMM without intervening late integration of hand shape. The approach is assessed in various ASLCR experimentation on data from two different large corpus datasets and two different sign languages: 1) German Sign Language: RWTH-PHOENIX-Weather for continuous German sign sentence data set consisting of 5356 weather related sentences, evaluated for Signer dependent, Cross-signer validation and Unseen signer Verification and 2) American Sign Language: ASLLVD consisting of more than 3300 isolated signs in continuous videos, also evaluated in three modes to prove the efficiency of namely Signer dependent, Cross-signer validation and Unseen signer Verification. In the experiments, signer dependent evaluations were carried out by taking single signer video per sign for training and the results were estimated. For cross-signer validation, two different samples of same sign from different signers were chosen and the results were calculated. Finally, for unseen signer verification the recognition accuracy was estimated against no overlapping data from training set. The training was done in the SU level lexica and the final testing experiment was done on the sign level via constructed SU lexica.

Extensive comparison experiments are conducted with four SU level approaches (Koller et al. 2015, Theodorakis et al. 2014, Bauer & Kraiss 2001, Cooper et al. 2012) and two whole-sign based approaches (Li et al. 2016, Dilsizian et al. 2014). The average results obtained for GSL corpus of RWTH-PHOENIX-Weather (304 sentences) with respect to other approaches shows an relative improvement of 6% from 2-S-U, 6.3% from SU-IMH, 12% from SU-noST and 12.3% from SU-F in cross-signer validation and for unseen signer verification, shows an relative improvement of 10.10% from SW-1. The average results obtained for ASLLVD of 3300 isolated signs with respect to other approaches shows an average improvement of 10.9% from 2-S-U, 29.3% from SU-noST, 26.3% from SU-F and 11.9% from SW-1. In conclusion, the overall framework produces effective recognition results when compared with other existing approaches and for large vocabulary data sets. Also, it has proved that the scalability of the system remains constant for increasing vocabulary of signs.

CHAPTER VII

7. Conclusion and Future Scope of Research Work

In this dissertation, the development of sophisticated techniques for modelling, training and recognizing the large vocabulary sign sentences are presented. This chapter concludes with the overall examination of this book, highlighting the contributions made and suggests some of the possible future directions in the research area of subunit modelling for automatic Sign Language Recognition. Section 7.1 gives the conclusion of proposed subunit sign modelling framework. Section 7.2 presents the future scope for extending the proposed research work.

7.1. Conclusion

In this dissertation, a novel and fully automatic Sign Language Recognition based on Subunit Sign modelling framework is introduced. This dissertation focused on solving the major issues and existing challenges of current SLR systems. The contributions of this book work focus on three important perspectives: (i) Feature Extraction and Selection, (ii) Handling Epentheses Movement Ambiguities and (iii) Automatic Recognition of Large Vocabulary Signs and Signer Adaptation.

i. The following conclusions were derived from the experimentation done on extracting manual and non-manual features for subunit sign modelling.

A novel Bayesian Parallel HMM is introduced to classify the manual and non-manual features of sign language. The proposed approach is evaluated subjectively using three different data sets collected from different sources which include ASLLVD for isolated and compound signs, RWTH-BOSTON-104 for continuous sentences and some self-captured videos of ASL alphabets and numbers. Experiments on four different dimensions based on ten-fold validation proved that the proposed approach produced an accuracy of 97.8% and 93.3% in the case of dependent signers for isolated and continuous sentences. Similarly, it shows an accuracy of 95.3% and 82.1% in the case of independent signers for isolated and continuous sentences. It shows an improvement of almost 18.6% when compared with generative feature selection methods and 9% improvement when compared with discriminative feature selection approaches for isolated and continuous signs respectively.

ii. The following conclusions were derived from the experimentation done on subunit modelling to handle epentheses movements and recognition ambiguities in sign language.

The proposed approach introduced Enhanced Dynamic Programming framework to solve the segmentation ambiguities in SLR. The proposed approach does not adopt any explicit or implicit modelling of epentheses movements. Instead, the epentheses movements between the adjacent signs are clustered and pruned dynamically by removing the sequence of last frames of preceding sign and the sequence of first frames of the succeeding sign. The EDP framework is implemented using spatiotemporal clustering which adapts Minimum Entropy Clustering to cluster spatial features and Dynamic Time Warping to cluster the temporal features.

Also, the proposed approach is evaluated experimentally in two aspects on three different data sets: First evaluation is done on identification of epentheses movements and the second evaluation is done to compare the proposed approach with other existing approaches. Based on the first evaluation, the system produces an accuracy of 98.6% in identifying the epentheses movements with 1% error rate variation for all three data sets. Similarly from the second experiment it is clearly noticed that when compared with other explicit and implicit models, the proposed EDP framework produces an average accuracy of 98.9% with the reduced error rate from 17% and 58% to 9% for HMM based approaches and CRF based approaches respectively.

iii. The following conclusions were derived from the experimentation done on Subunit sign modelling for sign language recognition from continuous sign sequences.

A novel subunit sign modelling framework () is introduced to recognize the large vocabulary isolated and continuous multimodal signs of different sign languages from unaided continuous video sequences. The BPaHMM, introduced in the dissertation, is used to model the spatial and temporal subunits. Based on Bakis topology, the sign lexicon is constructed for three subunits namely hand shape, position and velocity. The SMP-HMM is used for modelling the subunits and Viterbi algorithm and Baum-Welch algorithm are used to train and recognize the subunits.

The Subunit sign modelling framework was experimented on three different perspectives to prove the effectiveness of the proposed approach. First experiment was conducted on the basis of linguistic oriented and the data-driven oriented approaches. The proposed framework has shown the improvement of 16.4% error rate reduction when compared with other existing linguistic models. Second experiment was conducted to prove the efficiency of recognizing continuous sentences of large vocabularies and adapting the signer independencies. RWTH-PHOENIX-Weather dataset has been used to test the with four other existing approaches. The proposed approach shows around 91% and 88.1% average accuracies while gradually increasing the number of test sequences and cross-validating with signers. The final experiment was conducted to prove the system efficiency in recognizing isolated signs of large vocabularies and adapting the signer independencies. ASLLVD data set has been chosen to conduct the third experiment and compared with one sign based approach and three subunit based approaches. The proposed produced an accuracy of 99.3% and 97.3% for signer dependent and signer independent recognitions.

The proposed subunit sign modelling framework presented in this dissertation has contributed much to addressing and solving the three major challenges of automatic sign language recognition along with the concept of signer adaptation. Various experiments have been conducted to prove the effectiveness of the contributions of the proposed framework. From the experimental results, it is proved that the proposed approach is scalable and more reliable to extend to large vocabulary sign sequences. Also, it has been shown that the is cost effective and requires less computation time. The proposed framework has its own relaxation in handling all sorts of restrictions in the background, signer clothing and signer independence. Therefore, it is concluded that the proposed subunit sign modelling framework is efficient enough to adapt to the real world constraints and to recognize large vocabulary of sign under any circumstances.

7.2. Future Scope of Research Work

Major findings and conclusions have been reported in the dissertation. Some of the possible directions future work includes:

i. As a further enhancement, more non-standardized data will have two hands of different persons and hands of the differently abled persons will be included to establish the real-world system performance under different circumstances.

ii. As a possible future research direction, the proposed approach can be extended to act as natural gesture interface. Most of the current systems use mouse, keyboards or other input devices for feeding the input to the systems. All these devices are enough in attaining the efficiency of its designing needs. However, the applications of computers are evolving every day and there is a demand for natural gestural interfaces.

iii. In other ways, the proposed approach can be extended to human action analysis, motion modelling and recognition. It involves in recognizing human poses, actions and their activities in particular scenario.

References

[1] Admasu, YF & Raimond, K 2010, 'Ethiopian sign language recognition using Artificial Neural Network', IEEE 10th International Conference on Intelligent Systems Design and Applications (ISDA), pp. 995-1000.

[2] Agarwal, A & Thakur, MK 2013, 'Sign language recognition using Microsoft Kinect'. IEEE Sixth International Conference on Contemporary Computing (IC3), pp. 181-185.

[3] Ahmed, AA & Aly, S 2014, 'Appearance-based arabic sign language recognition using hidden markov models', IEEE International Conference on Engineering and Technology (ICET), pp. 1-6.

[4] Akmeliawati, R, Dadgostar, F, Demidenko, S, Gamage, N, Kuang, YC, Messom, C, Ooi, M, Sarrafzadeh, A, & SenGupta, G 2009, 'Towards real-time sign language analysis via markerless gesture tracking' IEEE Instrumentation and Measurement Technology Conference, pp. 1200-1204.

[5] Almeida, SG, Guimarães, FG & Ramírez, JA 2014, 'Feature extraction in Brazilian sign language recognition based on phonological structure and using RGB-D sensors' Expert Systems with Applications, vol. 41, no. 16, pp. 7259-7271.

[6] Al-Rousan, M, Assaleh, K & Tala'a, A 2009, 'Video-based signer-independent Arabic sign language recognition using hidden Markov models', Applied Soft Computing, vol. 9, no. 3, pp. 990-999.

[7] Al-Rousan, M, Al-Jarrah, O & Al-Hammouri, M 2010, 'Recognition of dynamic gestures in arabic sign language using two stages hierarchical scheme', International Journal of Knowledge-Based and Intelligent Engineering Systems, vol. 14, no.3, pp. 139-152.

[8] Anderson, R, Wiryana, F, Ariesta, MC & Kusuma, GP 2017, 'Sign Language Recognition Application Systems for Deaf-Mute People: A Review Based on Input-Process-Output', Procedia Computer Science, vol. 116, pp. 441-448.

[9] Appenrodt, J, Al-Hamadi, A & Michaelis, B 2010, 'Data gathering for gesture recognition systems based on single color-, stereo color-and thermal cameras', International Journal of Signal Processing, Image Processing and Pattern Recognition, vol. 3, no. 1, pp. 37-50.

[10] Aran, O, Burger, T, Caplier, A & Akarun, L 2007, 'Sequential belief-based fusion of manual and non-manual information for recognizing isolated signs', Springer International Gesture Workshop, pp. 134-144.

[11] Aran, O, Burger, T, Caplier, A & Akarun, L 2009, 'A belief-based sequential fusion approach for fusing manual signs and non-manual signals', Pattern Recognition, vol. 42, no. 5, pp. 812-822.

[12] Assaleh, K, Shanableh, T & Zourob, M 2012, 'Low complexity classification system for glove-based arabic sign language recognition', Springer Neural Information Processing, pp. 262-268.

[13] Athitsos, V & Sclaroff, S 2003, 'Estimating 3D hand pose from a cluttered image', IEEE Computer Society Conference on Computer Vision and Pattern Recognition, vol. 2, pp. 411-432.

[14] Baranwal, N & Nandi, GC 2017, 'An efficient gesture based humanoid learning using wavelet descriptor and MFCC techniques', International Journal of Machine Learning and Cybernetics, vol. 8, no. 4, pp. 1369-1388.

[15] Barros, PV, Júnior, NT, Bisneto, JM, Fernandes, BJ, Bezerra, BL & Fernandes, SM 2013, 'An effective dynamic gesture recognition system based on the feature vector reduction for SURF and LCS', Springer International Conference on Artificial Neural Networks, pp. 412-419.

[16] Bauer, B & Kraiss, KF 2001, 'Towards an automatic sign language recognition system using subunits', Proceedings of the Gesture workshop, pp. 64-75.

[17] Belgacem, S, Chatelain, C & Paquet, T 2017, 'Gesture sequence recognition with one shot learned CRF/HMM hybrid model', Image and Vision Computing, vol. 61, pp. 12-21.

[18] Bengio, Y & Frasconi, P 1996, 'Input-output HMMs for sequence processing', IEEE Transactions on Neural Networks, vol. 7, no.5, pp. 1231-1249.

[19] Bergasa, LM, Mazo, M, Gardel, A, Sotelo, MA & Boquete, L 2000, 'Unsupervised and adaptive Gaussian skin-color model', Image and Vision Computing, vol. 18, no. 12, pp. 987-1003.

[20] Berretti, S, Del, Bimbo, A & Pala, P 2013, 'Automatic facial expression recognition in real-time from dynamic sequences of 3D face scans', The Visual Computer, vol. 29, no. 12, pp. 1333-1350.

[21] Bilal, S, Akmeliawati, R, Salami, MJE & Shafie, AA 2015, 'Dynamic approach for real-time skin detection', Journal of Real-Time Image Processing, vol. 10, no. 2, pp. 371-385.

[22] Binh, Nguyen Dang & Toshiaki Ejima 2005, 'Hand gesture recognition using fuzzy neural network', In Proc. ICGST Conf. Graphics, Vision and Image Process, pp. 1-6.

[23] Bowden, R & Sarhadi, M 2002, 'A non-linear model of shape and motion for tracking finger spelt american sign language', Image and Vision Computing, vol. 20, no. 9, pp. 597-607.

[24] Brand, M, Oliver, N & Pentland, A 1997, 'Coupled hidden Markov models for complex action recognition' Proceedings of the IEEE Computer Society Conference on Computer vision and pattern recognition, pp. 994-999.

[25] Caridakis, G, Karpouzis, K, Drosopoulos, A & Kollias, S 2012, 'Non parametric, self organizing, scalable modeling of spatiotemporal inputs: The sign language paradigm', Neural Networks, vol. 36, 157-166.

[26] Caridakis, G, Asteriadis, S & Karpouzis, K 2014, 'Non-manual cues in automatic sign language recognition', Personal and ubiquitous computing, vol. 18, no. 1, pp. 37-46.

[27] Celebi, S, Aydin, AS, Temiz, TT & Arici, T 2013, 'Gesture Recognition using Skeleton Data with Weighted Dynamic Time Warping', InVISAPP, vol. 1, pp. 620-625.

[28] Chai, D & Ngan, KN 1999, 'Face segmentation using skin-color map in videophone applications', IEEE Transactions on circuits and systems for video technology, vol. 9, no. 4, pp. 551-564.

[29] Charles, D, Pedlow, K, McDonough, S, Shek, M & Charles, T 2013, 'An evaluation of the leap motion depth sensing camera for tracking hand and fingers motion in physical therapy', Interactive Technologies and Games Conference, vol. 1.

[30] Chen, Feng-Sheng, Chih-Ming Fu & Chung-Lin Huang 2003, 'Hand gesture recognition using a real-time tracking method and hidden Markov models', Image and vision computing, vol. 21, no. 8, pp. 745-758.

[31] Cho, OH & Lee, ST 2014, 'A study about honey bee dance serious game for kids using hand gesture', International Journal of Multimedia and Ubiquitous Engineering, vol. 9, no. 6, pp. 397-404.

[32] Chu, H, Ye, S, Guo, Q & Liu, X 2007, 'Object tracking algorithm based on camshift algorithm combinating with difference in frame', IEEE International Conference on Automation and Logistics, pp. 51-55.

[33] Chuan, CH, Regina, E & Guardino, C 2014, 'American sign language recognition using leap motion sensor', 13th International Conference on Machine Learning and Applications (ICMLA), pp. 541-544.

[34] Coogan, T & Sutherland, A 2006, 'Transformation invariance in hand shape recognition', 18th IEEE International Conference on Pattern Recognition (ICPR), vol. 3, pp. 485-488.

[35] Cooper, H & Bowden, R 2007, 'Sign language recognition using boosted volumetric features', Proceedings of the IAPR Conference on Machine Vision Applications, pp. 359-362.

[36] Cooper, H & Bowden, R 2010, 'Sign language recognition using linguistically derived sub-units', Proceedings of 4th workshop on the representation and processing of sign languages: corpora and sign language technologies, pp. 57-61.

[37] Cooper, H, Holt, B & Bowden, R 2011, 'Sign language recognition', Springer Journal of Visual Analysis of Humans, pp. 539-562.

[38] Cooper, H, Ong, EJ, Pugeault, N & Bowden, R 2012, 'Sign language recognition using sub-units', Journal of Machine Learning Research, pp. 2205-2231.

[39] Cooper, H, Ong, EJ, Pugeault, N & Bowden R, 'Sign Language Recognition Using Sub-units', Springer Gesture Recognition, pp. 89-118.

[40] Cootes, Timothy F, Gavin, V, Wheeler, Kevin N, Walker & Christopher JT 2000, 'Coupled-view active appearance models', Proceedings of the British machine vision conference, vol. 1, pp. 52-61.

[41] Cootes, TF, Edwards, GJ & Taylor, CJ 2001, 'Active appearance models', IEEE Transactions on pattern analysis and machine intelligence, vol. 23, no. 6, pp. 681-685.

[42] Cristinacce, D & Cootes, TF 2006, 'Feature Detection and Tracking with Constrained Local Models', BMVC, vol. 1, no. 2, pp. 3.

[43] Cui, Y & Weng, J 2000, 'Appearance-based hand sign recognition from intensity image sequences', Computer Vision and Image Understanding, vol. 78, no. 2, pp. 157-176.

[44] Dardas, NH & Georganas, ND 2011, 'Real-time hand gesture detection and recognition using bag-of-features and support vector machine techniques', IEEE Transactions on Instrumentation and Measurement, vol. 60, no. 11, pp. 3592-3607.

[45] Darrell, T & Pentland, A 1993, 'Space-time gestures', Proceedings of the IEEE Computer Society Conference on Computer Vision and Pattern Recognition, pp. 335-340.

[46] Deng, JW & Tsui, HT 2002, 'A novel two-layer PCA/MDA scheme for hand posture recognition', Proceedings of the 16th International Conference on Pattern Recognition, vol. 1, pp. 283-286.

[47] Deng, J & Tsui, HT 2002, 'A Two-step Approach based on PaHMM for the Recognition of ASL', The Fifth Asian Conference on Computer Vision (ACCV), pp. 1-6.

[48] Derpanis, KG, Wildes, RP & Tsotsos, JK 2008, 'Definition and recovery of kinematic features for recognition of American sign language movements', Image and Vision Computing, vol. 26, no. 12, pp. 1650-1662.

[49] Dilsizian, M, Yanovich, P, Wang, S, Neidle, C & Metaxas, DN 2014, 'A New Framework for Sign Language Recognition based on 3D Handshape Identification and Linguistic Modeling', LREC, pp. 1924-1929.

[50] Ding, L & Martinez, AM 2007, 'Recovering the linguistic components of the manual signs in american sign language', IEEE Conference on Advanced Video and Signal Based Surveillance, pp. 447-452.

[51] Dominio, F, Donadeo, M & Zanuttigh, P 2014, 'Combining multiple depth-based descriptors for hand gesture recognition', Pattern Recognition Letters, vol. 50, pp. 101-111.

[52] Dorner, B & Hagen, E 1994, 'Towards an american sign language interface', Artificial Intelligence Review, vol. 8, no.2-3, pp. 235-253.

[53] Dreuw, P, Deselaers, T, Rybach, D, Keysers, D & Ney, H 2006, 'Tracking using dynamic programming for appearance-based sign language recognition', 7th International Conference on Automatic Face and Gesture Recognition, pp. 293-298.

[54] Dreuw, P, Deselaers, T, Keysers, D & Ney, H 2006, 'Modeling image variability in appearance-based gesture recognition', ECCV Workshop on Statistical Methods in Multi-Image and Video Processing, pp. 7-18.

[55] Dreuw, P, Rybach, D, Deselaers, T, Zahedi, M & Ney, H 2007, 'Speech recognition techniques for a sign language recognition system', Proceedings of the International Conference on Speech Communication and Technology, vol. 60, no. 80, pp. 2513–2516.

[56] Dreuw, P, Forster, J, Deselaers, T & Ney, H 2008, 'Efficient approximations to model-based joint tracking and recognition of continuous sign language', 8th IEEE International Conference on Automatic Face & Gesture Recognition, pp. 1-6.

[57] El-Bendary, N, Zawbaa, HM, Daoud, MS, Hassanien, AE & Nakamatsu, K 2010, 'Arslat: Arabic sign language alphabets translator', International Conference on Computer Information Systems and Industrial Management Applications (CISIM), pp. 590-595.

[58] Elmezain, Mahmoud, Ayoub, Al-Hamadi & Bernd Michaelis 2008, 'Real-time capable system for hand gesture recognition using hidden markov models in stereo color image sequences', Journal of WSCG, pp. 65-72.

[59] Elmezain, M, Al-Hamadi, A, Appenrodt, J & Michaelis, B 2008, 'A hidden markov model-based continuous gesture recognition system for hand motion trajectory', 19th International Conference on Pattern Recognition, pp. 1-4.

[60] Elmezain, M, Al-Hamadi, A, Appenrodt, J & Michaelis, B 2009, 'A hidden markov model-based isolated and meaningful hand gesture recognition', International Journal of Electrical, Computer, and Systems Engineering, vol. 3, no.3, pp. 156-163.

[61] Elons, AS, Ahmed, M, Shedid, H & Tolba, MF 2014, 'Arabic sign language recognition using leap motion sensor', 9th International Conference on Computer Engineering & Systems (ICCES), pp. 368-373.

[62] Fang, G, Gao, X, Gao, W & Chen, Y 2004, 'A novel approach to automatically extracting basic units from chinese sign language', Proceedings of the 17th International Conference on Pattern Recognition, vol. 4, pp. 454-457.

[63] Fang, G, Gao, W & Zhao, D 2004, 'Large vocabulary sign language recognition based on fuzzy decision trees', IEEE Transactions on Systems, Man, and Cybernetics-Part A: Systems and Humans, vol. 34, no. 3, pp. 305-314.

[64] Fang, G, Gao, W & Zhao, D 2007, 'Large-vocabulary continuous sign language recognition based on transition-movement models', IEEE transactions on systems, man, and cybernetics-part a: systems and humans, vol. 37, no. 1, pp. 1-9.

[65] Fasel, B & Luettin, J 2003, 'Automatic facial expression analysis: a survey', Pattern recognition, vol. 36, no. 1, pp. 259-275.

[66] Feris, Rogerio, Matthew Turk, Ramesh Raskar, Karhan Tan & Gosuke Ohashi 2004, 'Exploiting depth discontinuities for vision-based fingerspelling recognition', IEEE Conference on Computer Vision and Pattern Recognition Workshop, pp. 155-155.

[67] Fok, KY, Cheng, CT & Ganganath, N 2015, 'Live demonstration: A hmm-based real-time sign language recognition system with multiple depth sensors', IEEE International Symposium on Circuits and Systems (ISCAS), pp. 1904-1904.

[68] Forster, J, Schmidt, C, Hoyoux, T, Koller, O, Zelle, U, Piater, JH &Ney, H 2012, 'RWTH-PHOENIX-Weather: A Large Vocabulary Sign Language Recognition and Translation Corpus', InLREC, pp. 3785-3789.

[69] Forster, J, Oberdörfer, C, Koller, O & Ney, H 2013, 'Modality combination techniques for continuous sign language recognition', Springer Iberian Conference on Pattern Recognition and Image Analysis, pp. 89-99.

[70] Forster, J, Schmidt, C, Koller, O, Bellgardt, M & Ney, H 2014, 'Extensions of the Sign Language Recognition and Translation Corpus RWTH-PHOENIX-Weather', InLREC, pp. 1911-1916.

[71] Gao, W, Fang, G, Zhao, D & Chen, Y 2004, 'A Chinese sign language recognition system based on SOFM/SRN/HMM', Pattern Recognition, vol. 37, no. 12, pp. 2389-2402.

[72] Ghahramani, Z & Jordan, MI 1996, 'Factorial hidden Markov models', Advances in Neural Information Processing Systems, pp. 472-478.

[73] Gianni, Frédérick, Christophe Collet & Patrice Dalle 2007, 'Robust tracking for processing of videos of communication's gestures' Springer International Gesture Workshop, pp. 93-101.

[74] Górecki, T & Łuczak, M 2015, 'Multivariate time series classification with parametric derivative dynamic time warping', Expert Systems with Applications, vol. 42, no. 5, pp. 2305-2312.

[75] Grobel, K & Assan, M 1997, 'Isolated sign language recognition using hidden Markov models', IEEE International Conference on Systems, Man, and Cybernetics, vol. 1, pp. 162-167.

[76] Grzeszcuk, R, Bradski, G, Chu, MH & Bouguet, JY 2000, 'Stereo based gesture recognition invariant to 3d pose and lighting', Proceedings of the IEEE Conference on Computer Vision and Pattern Recognition, vol. 1, pp. 826-833.

[77] Gupta, L & Ma, S 2001, 'Gesture-based interaction and communication: automated classification of hand gesture contours', IEEE Transactions on Systems, Man, and Cybernetics, Part C (Applications and Reviews), vol. 31, no. 1, pp.114-120.

[78] Gupta, N, Mittal, P, Roy, SD, Chaudhury, S & Banerjee, S 2002, 'Developing a gesture-based interface', IETE Journal of Research, vol. 48, no. 3-4, pp. 237-244.

[79] Habili, N, Lim, CC & Moini, A 2004, 'Segmentation of the face and hands in sign language video sequences using color and motion cues', IEEE Transactions on Circuits and Systems for Video Technology, vol. 14, no. 8, pp. 1086-1097.

[80] Hadfield, SJ & Bowden, R 2010, 'Generalised pose estimation using depth', Proceedings of the European Conference on Computer Vision (Workshops).

[81] Hamada, Y, Shimada, N & Shirai, Y 2004, 'Hand shape estimation under complex backgrounds for sign language recognition', Sixth IEEE International Conference on Automatic Face and Gesture Recognition, pp. 589-594.

[82] Han, J, Awad, G & Sutherland, A 2009, 'Automatic skin segmentation and tracking in sign language recognition', IET Computer Vision, vol. 3, no. 1, pp. 24-35.

[83] Han, Junwei, George Awad & Alistair Sutherland 2013, 'Boosted subunits: a framework for recognising sign language from videos', IET Image Processing, vol. 7, no. 1, pp. 70-80.

[84] Hanke T 2004, 'HamNoSys-representing sign language data in language resources and language processing contexts', LREC, vol. 4.

[85] Holden, EJ, Lee, G & Owens, R 2005, 'Australian sign language recognition', Machine Vision and Applications, vol. 16, no. 5, pp. 312.

[86] Holden, EJ & Owens, R 2010, 'Visual sign language recognition', Springer Multi-Image Analysis, pp. 270-287.

[87] Hongo, H, Ohya, M, Yasumoto, M, Niwa, Y & Yamamoto, K 2000, 'Focus of attention for face and hand gesture recognition using multiple cameras', Proceedings of the Fourth IEEE International Conference on Automatic Face and Gesture Recognition, pp. 156-161.

[88] Hopkins J 2008, 'Choosing how to write sign language: a sociolinguistic perspective', International Journal of the Sociology of Language, vol. 192, pp. 75-89.

[89] Hoshino K 2006, 'Dexterous robot hand control with data glove by human imitation', IEICE transactions on information and systems, vol. 89, no. 6, pp. 1820-1825.

[90] Huang CL, Huang WY. Sign language recognition using model-based tracking and a 3D Hopfield neural network. Machine vision and applications. 1998 Apr 18;10(5):292-307.

[91] Huang, CL & Jeng, SH 2001, 'A model-based hand gesture recognition system', Machine vision and applications, vol. 12, no. 5, pp. 243-258.

[92] Huang, S & Hong, J 2011, 'Moving object tracking system based on camshift and Kalman filter', International Conference on Consumer Electronics, Communications and Networks (CECNet), pp. 1423-1426.

[93] Ibrahim, NB, Selim, MM & Zayed, HH 2012, 'A dynamic skin detector based on face skin tone color', IEEE 8th International Conference on Informatics and Systems (INFOS), pp. 1-5.

[94] Ibrahim, NB, Selim, MM & Zayed, HH 2017, 'An Automatic Arabic Sign Language Recognition System (ArSLRS)', Journal of King Saud University-Computer and Information Sciences.

[95] Jiang, F, Gao, W, Yao, H, Zhao, D & Chen, X 2009, 'Synthetic data generation technique in Signer-independent sign language recognition', Pattern Recognition Letters, vol. 30, no. 5, pp. 513-524.

[96] Jian-zheng, L & Zheng, Z 2011, 'Head movement recognition based on LK algorithm and Gentleboost', IEEE 7th International Conference on InNetworked Computing and Advanced Information Management (NCM), pp. 232-236.

[97] Jurafsky, D & Martin, JH 2014, 'Speech and language processing', Pearson.

[98] Just, A, Bernier, O & Marcel, S 2004, 'HMM and IOHMM for the recognition of mono-and bi-manual 3D hand gestures', Institut Dalle Molle d'Intelligence Artificielle Perceptive (IDIAP).

[99] Kadir, T, Bowden, R, Ong, EJ & Zisserman, A 2004, 'Minimal Training, Large Lexicon, Unconstrained Sign Language Recognition', British Machine Vision Conference, pp. 1-10.

[100] Kanaujia, A, Huang, Y & Metaxas, D 2006, 'Tracking facial features using mixture of point distribution models', Computer Vision, Graphics and Image Processing, pp. 492-503.

[101] Kapuscinski, T, Oszust, M, Wysocki, M & Warchol, D 2015, 'Recognition of hand gestures observed by depth cameras', International Journal of Advanced Robotic Systems, 2015, vol. 12, no. 4, pp. 36.

[102] Karami, A, Zanj, B & Sarkaleh, AK 2011, 'Persian sign language (PSL) recognition using wavelet transform and neural networks', Expert Systems with Applications, vol. 38, no. 3, pp. 2661-2667.

[103] Kawulok M 2008, 'Dynamic skin detection in color images for sign language recognition', Image and Signal Processing, pp. 112-119.

[104] Kelly, Daniel, Jane Reilly Delannoy, John McDonald & Charles Markham 2009, 'Automatic recognition of head movement gestures in sign language sentences', Proceedings of the 4th China-Ireland Information and Communications Technologies Conference, pp. 142-145.

[105] Kelly, D, McDonald, J & Markham, C 2011, 'Recognition of spatiotemporal gestures in sign language using gesture threshold hmms', Machine Learning for Vision-Based Motion Analysis, pp. 307-348.

[106] Keskin, C & Akarun, L 2009, 'STARS: Sign tracking and recognition system using input–output HMMs', Pattern Recognition Letters, vol. 30, no. 12, pp. 1086-1095.

[107] Keskin, C, Kıraç F, Kara, YE & Akarun, L 2012, 'Hand pose estimation and hand shape classification using multi-layered randomized decision forests', Springer European Conference on Computer Vision, pp. 852-863.

[108] Khademi, M, Mousavi Hondori, H, McKenzie, A, Dodakian, L, Lopes, CV & Cramer, SC 2014, 'Free-hand interaction with leap motion controller for stroke rehabilitation', Proceedings of the extended abstracts of the 32nd annual ACM conference on Human factors in computing systems, pp. 1663-1668.

[109] Kim, Jong-Sung, Won Jang & Zeungnam Bien 1996, 'A dynamic gesture recognition system for the Korean sign language (KSL)', IEEE Transactions on Systems, Man, and Cybernetics, Part B (Cybernetics), vol. 26, no. 2, pp. 354-359.

[110] Kim, T, Keane, J, Wang, W, Tang, H, Riggle, J, Shakhnarovich, G, Brentari, D & Livescu, K 2017, 'Lexicon-Free Fingerspelling Recognition from Video: Data, Models, and Signer Adaptation', Computer Speech & Language.

[111] Kirac, F, Kara, YE & Akarun, L 2014, 'Hierarchically constrained 3D hand pose estimation using regression forests from single frame depth data', Pattern Recognition Letters, vol. 50, pp. 91-100.

[112] Kriegel, HP, Schubert, E & Zimek, A 2017, 'The (black) art of runtime evaluation: Are we comparing algorithms or implementations?', Knowledge and Information Systems, vol. 52, no. 2, pp. 341-378.

[113] Koller, O, Ney, H & Bowden, R 2013, 'May the force be with you: Force-aligned signwriting for automatic subunit annotation of corpora', 10th IEEE International Conference and Workshops on Automatic Face and Gesture Recognition (FG), pp. 1-6.

[114] Koller, O, Forster, J & Ney, H 2015, 'Continuous sign language recognition: Towards large vocabulary statistical recognition systems handling multiple signers', Computer Vision and Image Understanding, vol. 141, pp. 108-125.

[115] Koller, O, Bowden, R & Ney, H 2016, 'Automatic Alignment of HamNoSys Subunits for Continuous Sign Language Recognition', Proceedings of the 7th Workshop on the Representation and Processing of Sign Languages: Corpus Mining, Portorož, Slovenia, LREC, pp. 121-128.

[116] Kong, WW & Ranganath, S 2014, 'Towards subject independent continuous sign language recognition: A segment and merge approach', Pattern Recognition, vol. 47, no. 3, pp. 1294-1308.

[117] Kumar, P, Gauba, H, Roy, PP & Dogra, DP 2017, 'A multimodal framework for sensor based sign language recognition', Neurocomputing, vol. 259, pp. 21-38.

[118] Kumar, P, Roy, PP & Dogra, DP 2018, 'Independent Bayesian classifier combination based sign language recognition using facial expression', Information Sciences, vol. 428, pp. 30-48.

[119] Kurdyumov, Ruslan, Phillip Ho & Justin, Ng 2011, 'Sign Language Classification Using Webcam Images', pp. 1-4.

[120] Lai, K, Konrad, J & Ishwar, P 2012, 'A gesture-driven computer interface using Kinect', IEEE Southwest Symposium on Image Analysis and Interpretation (SSIAI), pp. 185-188.

[121] Lang, S, Block, M & Rojas, R 2012, 'Sign language recognition using kinect', Artificial intelligence and soft computing, pp. 394-402.

[122] Li, K, Zhou, Z & Lee, CH 2016, 'Sign transition modeling and a scalable solution to continuous sign language recognition for real-world applications', ACM Transactions on Accessible Computing (TACCESS), vol. 8, no. 2, pp. 7-23.

[123] Li, YB, Shen, XL & Bei, SS 2011, 'Real-time tracking method for moving target based on an improved Camshift algorithm', International Conference on Mechatronic Science, Electric Engineering and Computer (MEC), pp. 978-981.

[124] Li, H, Zhang, K & Jiang, T 2004, 'Minimum Entrophy Clustering and Applications to Gene Expression Analysis', 3rd IEEE Computational Systems Bioinformatics Conference, pp. 142-151.

[125] Lichtenauer, JF, Hendriks, EA & Reinders, MJ 2008, 'Sign language recognition by combining statistical DTW and independent classification', IEEE Transactions on Pattern Analysis and Machine Intelligence, vol. 30, no. 11, pp. 2040-2046.

[126] Liddell, SK & Johnson, RE 1989, 'American sign language: The phonological base', Sign language studies, vol. 64, no. 1, pp. 195-277.

[127] Liu, N & Lovell, BC 2003, 'Gesture classification using hidden markov models and viterbi path counting', seventh Digital image computing: techniques and Applications, pp. 273-282.

[128] Marcel, S, Bernier, O, Viallet, JE & Collobert, D 2000, 'Hand gesture recognition using input-output hidden markov models', Proceedings of the Fourth IEEE International Conference on Automatic Face and Gesture Recognition, pp. 456-461.

[129] Marin, G, Dominio, F & Zanuttigh, P 2014, 'Hand gesture recognition with leap motion and kinect devices', IEEE International Conference on Image Processing (ICIP), pp. 1565-1569.

[130] Marin, G, Dominio, F & Zanuttigh, P 2016, 'Hand gesture recognition with jointly calibrated Leap Motion and depth sensor', Multimedia Tools and Applications, vol. 75, no. 22, pp. 14991-5015.

[131] Mehrotra, K, Godbole, A & Belhe, S 2015, 'Indian Sign Language Recognition Using Kinect Sensor', Springer International Conference Image Analysis and Recognition, pp. 528-535.

[132] Metaxas, DN, Liu, B, Yang, F, Yang, P, Michael, N & Neidle, C 2012, 'Recognition of Nonmanual Markers in American Sign Language (ASL) Using Non-Parametric Adaptive 2D-3D Face Tracking', Proceedings of Language Resources and Evaluation Conference, pp. 2414-2420.

[133] Mohandes, M, Aliyu, S & Deriche, M 2014, 'Arabic sign language recognition using the leap motion controller', IEEE 23rd International Symposium on Industrial Electronics (ISIE), pp. 960-965.

[134] Mohandes, M, A-Buraiky, S, Halawani, T & Al-Baiyat, S 2004, 'Automation of the Arabic sign language recognition', Proceedings of the IEEE International Conference on In Information and Communication Technologies: From Theory to Applications, pp. 479-480.

[135] Mohandes, M, Deriche, M, Johar, U & Ilyas, S 2012, 'A signer-independent Arabic Sign Language recognition system using face detection, geometric features, and a Hidden Markov Model', Computers & Electrical Engineering, vol. 38, no. 2, pp. 422-433.

[136] Molchanov, P, Gupta, S, Kim, K & Kautz, J 2015, 'Hand gesture recognition with 3D convolutional neural networks', Proceedings of the IEEE conference on computer vision and pattern recognition workshops, pp. 1-7.

[137] Murakami, K & Taguchi, H 1991, 'Gesture recognition using recurrent neural networks', Proceedings of the ACM SIGCHI conference on Human factors in computing systems, pp. 237-242.

[138] Murphy-Chutorian, E & Trivedi, MM 2009, 'Head pose estimation in computer vision: A survey', IEEE transactions on pattern analysis and machine intelligence', vol. 31, no. 4, pp. 607-626.

[139] Nandy, A, Prasad, JS, Mondal, S, Chakraborty, P & Nandi, GC 2010, 'Recognition of isolated indian sign language gesture in real time', Information Processing and Management, pp. 102-107.

[140] Nam, Y & Wohn, K 1996, 'Recognition of space-time hand-gestures using hidden Markov model', ACM symposium on Virtual reality software and technology, pp. 51-58.

[141] Nam, Y, Wohn, N & Lee-Kwang, H 1999, 'Modeling and recognition of hand gesture using colored Petri nets', IEEE Transactions on Systems, Man, and Cybernetics-Part A: Systems and Humans, vol. 29, no. 5, pp. 514-521.

[142] Neidle, C, Thangali, A & Sclaroff, S 2012, 'Challenges in development of the american sign language lexicon video dataset (ASLLVD) corpus', Proceedings of the 5th Workshop on the Representation and Processing of Sign Languages: Interactions between Corpus and Lexicon.

[143] Neidle, C, Liu, J, Liu, B, Peng, X, Vogler, C & Metaxas, D 2014, 'Computer-based tracking, analysis, and visualization of linguistically significant nonmanual events in American Sign Language (ASL)', LREC Workshop on the Representation and Processing of Sign Languages: Beyond the Manual Channel, vol. 5.

[144] Nguyen, Tan Dat & Surendra Ranganath 2008, 'Tracking facial features under occlusions and recognizing facial expressions in sign language', IEEE 8th International onference on Automatic Face & Gesture Recognition, pp. 1-7.

[145] Nolker, C & Ritter, H 2002, 'Visual recognition of continuous hand postures', IEEE Transactions on neural networks, vol. 13, no. 4, pp. 983-994.

[146] Ong, SC & Ranganath, S 2004, 'Deciphering gestures with layered meanings and signer adaptation', Sixth IEEE International Conference on Automatic Face and Gesture Recognition, pp. 559-564.

[147] Ong, SC & Ranganath, S 2005, 'Automatic sign language analysis: A survey and the future beyond lexical meaning', IEEE Transactions on Pattern Analysis & Machine Intelligence, vol. 1, no. 6, pp. 873-891.

[148] Ong, EJ, Cooper, H, Pugeault, N & Bowden, R 2012, 'Sign language recognition using sequential pattern trees', IEEE Conference on Computer Vision and Pattern Recognition (CVPR), pp. 2200-2207.

[149] Ong, EJ, Koller, O, Pugeault, N & Bowden, R 2014, 'Sign spotting using hierarchical sequential patterns with temporal intervals', Proceedings of the IEEE Conference on Computer Vision and Pattern Recognition, pp. 1923-1930.

[150] Ouhyoung, M & Liang, RH 1996, 'A sign language recognition system using hidden markov model and context sensitive search', Proceedings of ACM Virtual Reality Software and Technology Conference, pp. 59-66.

[151] Oz, C & Leu, MC 2011, 'American Sign Language word recognition with a sensory glove using artificial neural networks', Engineering Applications of Artificial Intelligence, vol. 24, no. 7, pp. 1204-1213.

[152] Oszust, M & Wysocki, M 2012, 'Modelling and Recognition of Signed Expressions Using Subunits Obtained by Data-Driven Approach', International Conference on Artificial Intelligence: Methodology, Systems, and Applications, pp. 315-324.

[153] Oszust, M & Wysocki, M 2013, 'Polish sign language words recognition with kinect', IEEE 6th International Conference on Human System Interaction (HSI), pp. 219-226.

[154] Oszust, M & Wysocki, M 2014, 'Some Approaches to Recognition of Sign Language Dynamic Expressions with Kinect', Springer Human-Computer Systems Interaction: Backgrounds and Applications, vol. 3, pp. 75-86.

[155] Ouhyoung, M & Liang, RH 1996, 'A sign language recognition system using hidden markov model and context sensitive search', Proceedings of ACM Virtual Reality Software and Technology Conference, pp. 59-66.

[156] Palacios, JM, Sagüés, C, Montijano, E & Llorente, S 2013, 'Human-computer interaction based on hand gestures using RGB-D sensors', Sensors, vol. 13, no. 9, pp. 11842-11860.

[157] Pattanaworapan, K & Chamnongthai, K 2012, 'Finger alphabet recognition for automatic sign language interpretation system', 35th Electrical Engineering Conference (EECON35), pp. 12-14.

[158] Pattanaworapan, K, Chamnongthai, K & Guo, JM 2016, 'Signer-independence finger alphabet recognition using discrete wavelet transform and area level run lengths', Journal of Visual Communication and Image Representation, vol. 38, pp. 658-677.

[159] Pedersoli, F, Benini, S, Adami, N & Leonardi, R 2014, 'XKin: an open source framework for hand pose and gesture recognition using kinect', The Visual Computer, vol. 30, no. 10, pp. 1107-1122.

[160] Pitsikalis, V, Theodorakis, S, Vogler, C & Maragos, P 2011, 'Advances in phonetics-based sub-unit modeling for transcription alignment and sign language recognition', IEEE Computer Society Conference on Computer Vision and Pattern Recognition Workshops (CVPRW), pp. 1-6.

[161] Potter, LE, Araullo, J & Carter, L 2013, 'The leap motion controller: a view on sign language', Proceedings of the ACM 25th Australian computer-human interaction conference: augmentation, application, innovation, collaboration, pp. 175-178.

[162] Pugeault, N & Bowden, R 2011, 'Spelling it out: Real-time asl fingerspelling recognition', IEEE International Conference on Computer Vision Workshops (ICCV Workshops), pp. 1114-1119.

[163] Raheja, JL, Chaudhary, A & Singal, K 2011, 'Tracking of fingertips and centers of palm using kinect', IEEE third international conference on Computational intelligence, modelling and simulation (CIMSiM), pp. 248-252.

[164] Rao, DV, Patil, S, Babu, NA & Muthukumar, V 2006, 'Implementation and evaluation of image processing algorithms on reconfigurable architecture using C-based hardware descriptive languages', International Journal of Theoretical and Applied Computer Sciences, vol. 1, no. 1, pp. 9-34.

[165] Reale, M, Liu, P & Yin, L 2011, 'Using eye gaze, head pose, and facial expression for personalized non-player character interaction', IEEE Computer Society Conference on Computer Vision and Pattern Recognition Workshops (CVPRW), pp. 13-18.

[166] Rekha, J, Bhattacharya, J & Majumder, S 2011, 'Hand gesture recognition for sign language: A new hybrid approach', International Conference on Image Processing, Computer Vision, and Pattern Recognition (IPCV), pp. 80-86.

[167] Rekha, J, Bhattacharya, J & Majumder, S 2011, 'Shape, texture and local movement hand gesture features for indian sign language recognition', IEEE 3rd International Conference on Trendz in Information Sciences and Computing (TISC), pp. 30-35.

[168] Reyes, M, Domínguez, G & Escalera, S 2011, 'Featureweighting in dynamic timewarping for gesture recognition in depth data', IEEE International Conference on Computer Vision Workshops (ICCV Workshops), pp. 1182-1188.

[169] Rezaei, A, Vafadoost, M, Rezaei, S & Daliri, A 2008, '3D pose estimation via elliptical fourier descriptors for deformable hand representations', IEEE 2nd International Conference on Bioinformatics and Biomedical Engineering, pp. 1871-1875.

[170] Riviere, J & Guitton, P 2004, 'Real time model based tracking using silhouette features', Proceedings of RFIA, Toulouse, France.

[171] Rossol, N, Cheng, I & Basu, A 2016, 'A multisensor technique for gesture recognition through intelligent skeletal pose analysis', IEEE Transactions on Human-Machine Systems, vol. 46, no. 3, pp. 350-359.

[172] Roussos, A, Theodorakis, S, Pitsikalis, V & Maragos, P 2010, 'Hand Tracking and Affine Shape-Appearance Handshape Sub-units in Continuous Sign Language Recognition', ECCV Workshops, vol. 1, pp. 258-272.

[173] Rudovic, O, Pavlovic, V & Pantic, M 2012, 'Multi-output laplacian dynamic ordinal regression for facial expression recognition and intensity estimation', IEEE Conference on Computer Vision and Pattern Recognition (CVPR), pp. 2634-2641.

[174] Salmond, DJ, & Birch, H 2001, 'A particle filter for track-before-detect, Proceedings of the IEEE American Control Conference, vol. 5, pp. 3755-3760.

[175] Schmitt, D & McCoy, N 2011, 'Object classification and localization using SURF descriptors', CS, vol. 229, pp. 1-5.

[176] Shanableh, T, Assaleh, K & Al-Rousan, M 2017, 'Spatio-temporal feature-extraction techniques for isolated gesture recognition in Arabic sign language', IEEE Transactions on Systems, Man, and Cybernetics, Part B (Cybernetics), vol. 37, no. 3, pp. 641-650.

[177] Sherrah, J & Gong, S 2000, 'Resolving Visual Uncertainty and Occlusion through Probabilistic Reasoning', British Machine Vision Conference, pp. 1-10.

[178] Shukor, AZ, Miskon, MF, Jamaluddin, MH, bin Ali, F, Asyraf, MF, & bin Bahar, MB 2015, 'A new data glove approach for Malaysian sign language detection', Procedia Computer Science, vol. 76, pp. 60-67.

[179] Starner, T, Weaver, J & Pentland, A 1998, 'Real-time american sign language recognition using desk and wearable computer based video', IEEE Transactions on Pattern Analysis and Machine Intelligence, vol. 20, no. 12, pp. 1371-1375.

[180] Stenger B 2006, 'Template-based hand pose recognition using multiple cues', Computer Vision–ACCV, pp.551-560.

[181] Stokoe, WC, Casterline, DC & Croneberg, CG 1976, 'A dictionary of American Sign Language on linguistic principles', Linstok Press.

[182] Stokoe WC 1991, 'Semantic phonology', Sign Language Studies, vol. 71, no. 1, pp. 107-114.

[183] Stokoe William C 2005, 'Sign language structure: An outline of the visual communication systems of the American deaf', Journal of deaf studies and deaf education, vol. 10, no. 1, pp. 3-37.

[184] Suarez, J & Murphy, RR 2012, 'Hand gesture recognition with depth images: A review', IEEE Ro-man, pp. 411-417.

[185] Sadek, MI, Mikhael, MN & Mansour, HA 2017, 'A new approach for designing a smart glove for Arabic Sign Language Recognition system based on the statistical analysis of the Sign Language', 34th National Radio Science Conference (NRSC), pp. 380-388.

[186] Sun, Q, Liu, H, Liu, M & Zhang, T 2016, 'Human activity prediction by mapping grouplets to recurrent Self-Organizing Map', Neurocomputing, vol. 177, pp. 427-440.

[187] Supalla, SJ, McKee, C & Cripps, JH 2014, 'An overview on the ASL-phabet', Tucson, AZ: Gloss Institute.

[188] Sutton V 2000, 'Sign writing', DAC f. S. Writing.

[189] Tanibata, N, Shimada, N & Shirai, Y 2002, 'Extraction of hand features for recognition of sign language words', International conference on vision interface, pp. 391-398.

[190] Thangali, A, Nash, JP, Sclaroff, S & Neidle, C 2011, 'Exploiting phonological constraints for handshape inference in ASL video', IEEE Conference on Computer Vision and Pattern Recognition (CVPR), pp. 521-528.

[191] Tharwat, A, Gaber, T, Hassanien, AE, Shahin, MK & Refaat, B 2015, 'Sift-based arabic sign language recognition system', Springer Afro-european conference for industrial advancement, pp. 359-370.

[192] Theodorakis, S, Katsamanis, A & Maragos, P 2009, 'Product-HMMs for automatic sign language recognition', IEEE International Conference on Acoustics, Speech and Signal Processing, pp. 1601-1604.

[193] Theodorakis S, Pitsikalis V, Maragos P. Model-level data-driven sub-units for signs in videos of continuous sign language. InAcoustics Speech and Signal Processing (ICASSP), 2010 IEEE International Conference on 2010 Mar 14 (pp. 2262-2265). IEEE.

[194] Theodorakis, S, Pitsikalis, V & Maragos, P 2014, 'Dynamic–static unsupervised sequentiality, statistical subunits and lexicon for sign language recognition', Image and Vision Computing, vol. 32, no. 8, pp. 533-549.

[195] Tian, Ying-Li, Takeo Kanade & Jeffrey, F. Cohn 2005, 'Facial expression analysis', Handbook of face recognition, pp. 247-275.

[196] Tubaiz, N, Shanableh, T & Assaleh, K 2015, 'Glove-based continuous Arabic sign language recognition in user-dependent mode', IEEE Transactions on Human-Machine Systems, vol. 45, no. 4, pp. 526-533.

[197] Unanue, IJ, Borzeshi, EZ & Piccardi, M 2017, 'Recurrent neural networks with specialized word embeddings for health-domain named-entity recognition', Journal of biomedical informatics, vol. 76, pp. 102-109.

[198] Vamsikrishna, KM, Debi Prosad Dogra & Maunendra Sankar Desarkar, 'Computer-Vision-Assisted Palm Rehabilitation With Supervised Learning', IEEE Transactions on Biomedical Engineering, vol. 63, no. 5, pp. 991-1001.

[199] Valstar, MF & Pantic, M 2012, 'Fully automatic recognition of the temporal phases of facial actions', IEEE Transactions on Systems, Man, and Cybernetics, Part B (Cybernetics), vol. 42, no. 1, pp. 28-43.

[200] Vogler, C & Metaxas, D 1997, 'Adapting hidden Markov models for ASL recognition by using three-dimensional computer vision methods', IEEE International Conference on Systems, Man, and Cybernetics, 1997, vol. 1, pp. 156-161.

[201] Vogler, C & Metaxas, D 1999, 'Parallel hidden markov models for american sign language recognition', Proceedings of the Seventh IEEE International Conference on Computer Vision, vol. 1, pp. 116-122.

[202] Vogler, C & Metaxas, D 2001, 'A framework for recognizing the simultaneous aspects of american sign language', Computer Vision and Image Understanding, vol. 81, no. 3, pp. 358-384.

[203] Vogler C & Metaxas D 2004, 'Handshapes and Movements: Multiple-Channel ASL Recognition', Lecture Notes in Artificial Intelligence, vol. 2915, pp. 247-258.

[204] Vogler, C, Li, Z, Kanaujia, A, Goldenstein, S & Metaxas D 2007, 'The best of both worlds: Combining 3d deformable models with active shape models', IEEE 11th International Conference on Computer Vision, pp. 1-7.

[205] Von Agris, U, Zieren, J, Canzler, U, Bauer, B & Kraiss, KF 2008, 'Recent developments in visual sign language recognition', Universal Access in the Information Society, vol. 6, no. 4, pp. 323-362.

[206] Von Agris, U, Knorr, M & Kraiss KF 2008, 'The significance of facial features for automatic sign language recognition', 8th IEEE International Conference on Automatic Face & Gesture Recognition, pp. 1-6.

[207] Waldron, MB & Kim, S 1995, 'Isolated ASL sign recognition system for deaf persons', IEEE Transactions on rehabilitation engineering, vol. 3, no. 3, pp. 261-271.

[208] Wang, C, Chen, X & Gao, W 2006, 'Expanding training set for chinese sign language recognition', 7th International Conference on Automatic Face and Gesture Recognition, pp. 323-328.

[209] Wang, F & Lin, Y 2009, 'Improving particle filter with a new sampling strategy', IEEE 4th International Conference on Computer Science & Education, pp. 408-412.

[210] Wang, RY & Popović, J 2009, 'Real-time hand-tracking with a color glove', ACM transactions on graphics (TOG), vol. 28, no. 3, p. 63.

[211] Wen, Y, Hu, C, Yu, G & Wang, C 2012, 'A robust method of detecting hand gestures using depth sensors', IEEE International Workshop on Haptic Audio Visual Environments and Games (HAVE), pp. 72-77.

[212] Wilson, AD & Bobick, AF 1999, 'Parametric hidden markov models for gesture recognition', IEEE transactions on pattern analysis and machine intelligence, vol. 21, no. 9, pp. 884-900.

[213] Wong, SF & Cipolla, R 2005, 'Real-time adaptive hand motion recognition using a sparse bayesian classifier', ICCV Workshop on Computer Vision in Human-Computer Interaction, pp. 170-179.

[214] Yang, HD, Sclaroff, S & Lee, SW 2009, 'Sign language spotting with a threshold model based on conditional random fields', IEEE Transactions on Pattern Analysis and Machine Intelligence, vol .31, no. 7, pp. 1264-1277.

[215] Yang, HD & Lee, SW 2013, 'Robust sign language recognition by combining manual and non-manual features based on conditional random field and support vector machine', Pattern Recognition Letters, vol. 34, no. 16, pp. 2051-2056.

[216] Yang, Ming-Hsuan, Narendra Ahuja & Mark Tabb 2002, 'Extraction of 2d motion trajectories and its application to hand gesture recognition', IEEE Transactions on pattern analysis and machine intelligence, vol. 24, no. 8, pp. 1061-1074.

[217] Yang, R, Sarkar, S & Loeding, B 2010, 'Handling movement epenthesis and hand segmentation ambiguities in continuous sign language recognition using nested dynamic programming', IEEE transactions on pattern analysis and machine intelligence, vol. 32, no. 3, pp. 462-477.

[218] Yang, W, Tao, J & Ye, Z 2016, 'Continuous sign language recognition using level building based on fast hidden Markov model', Pattern Recognition Letters, vol. 78, pp. 28-35.

[219] Yeasin, M & Chaudhuri, S 2000, 'Visual understanding of dynamic hand gestures', Pattern Recognition, vol. 33, no. 11, pp. 1805-1817.

[220] Yilmaz, A, Javed, O & Shah, M 2006, 'Object tracking: A survey', ACM Computing Surveys (CSUR), vol. 38, no. 4, pp. 13.

[221] Yin, P, Starner, T, Hamilton, H, Essa, I & Rehg, JM 2009, 'Learning the basic units in american sign language using discriminative segmental feature selection', IEEE International Conference on Acoustics, Speech and Signal Processing, pp. 4757-4760.

[222] Yu, C, Wang, X, Huang, H, Shen, J & Wu, K 2010, 'Vision-based hand gesture recognition using combinational features', Sixth International Conference on Intelligent Information Hiding and Multimedia Signal Processing (IIH-MSP), pp. 543-546.

[223] Yuan, Q, Geo, W, Yao, H & Wang, C 2002, 'Recognition of strong and weak connection models in continuous sign language', Proceedings of the 16th IEEE International Conference on InPattern Recognition, 2002. vol. 1, pp. 75-78.

[224] Zahedi M, Dreuw P, Rybach D, Deselaers T, Ney H. Geometric Features for Improving Continuous Appearance-based Sign Language Recognition. InBMVC 2006 (Vol. 3, pp. 1019-1028).

[225] Zahedi, M, Keysers, D, Deselaers, T & Ney, H 2005, 'Combination of tangent distance and an image distortion model for appearance-based sign language recognition', Lecture notes in computer science, vol. 3663, pp. 401.

[226] Zaki, MM & Shaheen, SI 2011, 'Sign language recognition using a combination of new vision based features', Pattern Recognition Letters, vol. 32(4), 572-577.

[227] Zhang, H, Wang, Y & Deng, C 2011, 'Application of gesture recognition based on simulated annealing bp neural network', IEEE IEEE International Conference on Electronic and Mechanical Engineering and Information Technology (EMEIT), vol. 1, pp. 178-181).

[228] Zhang, X, Chen, X, Li, Y, Lantz, V, Wang, K & Yang, J 2011, 'A framework for hand gesture recognition based on accelerometer and EMG sensors', IEEE Transactions on Systems, Man, and Cybernetics-Part A: Systems and Humans, vol. 41, no. 6, pp. 1064-1076.

[229] Zhao, X & Zhang, S 2011, 'Facial expression recognition based on local binary patterns and kernel discriminant isomap', Sensors, vol. 11, no. 10, pp. 9573-9588.

[230] Zieren, J, Unger, N & Akyol, S 2002, 'Hands tracking from frontal view for vision-based gesture recognition', Pattern Recognition, pp. 531-539.

[231] Zieren, J & Kraiss, KF 2005, 'Robust person-independent visual sign language recognition', Pattern recognition and image analysis, pp. 333-355.